BIZNISTRY

Transforming Lives
Through Enterprise

Jeff Greer
Chuck Proudfit

P5 Publications

Mason, Ohio

BIZNISTRY®: Transforming Lives Through Enterprise
©2013 by Jeff Greer and Chuck Proudfit

P5 Publications
406 Fourth Avenue
Mason, Ohio 45040
United States of America

Contents

Biznistry Profiles:

Introduction: Colliding Worlds

"Hey! You got your peanut butter on my chocolate!"
"You got your chocolate in my peanut butter!"

In a classic 1980 TV ad for Reese's Peanut Butter Cups, a guy strolls down the sidewalk, sinking his teeth into a sweet, creamy bar of chocolate. Another guy approaches from around the corner, scooping peanut butter from the jar with his finger. Bam! They collide at the intersection, and their snacks collide as well. Indignant at first, the two taste the new combination and declare, "This is good . . . this is *really* good!"[1]

This book is about two disciplines, both useful, both respected, that have long been kept separate: business and ministry. Business appeals to the head—planning, calculating, implementing—its goal clear: provide a product or service people want, and make as much money as you can. Ministry appeals to the heart—loving, sacrificing, serving—its goal to do God's will, not always so clear. Ministry is done by pastors and missionaries and once in a while by Christians when they have time outside their normal schedules. Business is for the rest of us who need to earn our living through "secular" work.

The world of business—the marketplace—usually sees ministry as something best left to the institutional church, performed over the weekends and inside church walls. It steers away from even discussing the "inflammatory" topics of religion and politics. It tends to partition church and work in formal policy, written law and unstated expectation. Keep your chocolate out of my peanut butter.

Meanwhile, to many in ministry, the marketplace is a "worldly" environment polluted with greed and corruption, and filled with unfamiliar terms and approaches. Passionate to enlarge and serve the Kingdom of God, those in ministry are suspicious of business practices they fear would compromise their faith and quench the Spirit's leading. Keep your peanut butter off my chocolate.

Since you are reading this, you probably feel at some deep level that maybe there is an alternative to this separated world. Is it possible that combining two good things—business and ministry—can produce something even better? This book will introduce you to some ordinary people who have discovered that the integration of business and ministry—what we call Biznistry®— creates a synergy that is not only "really good," but also changes lives and impacts the world.

Our story starts in the middle. We did not invent the practice of marketplace ministry, nor do we pretend to have the definitive word on all it can be. Along our journey we have discovered that marketplace and ministry often enjoyed a close relationship in Old and New Testament days, and in bright spots small and large throughout history. Today, Christians usually see the marketplace as a means to fund ministry, rather than to do ministry. But faith-based work ministries and Christ-centered enterprises are springing up and multiplying. As we write this, people all over the world are finding new ways to expand God's Kingdom in the work world. Biznistry is just one type of faith-based marketplace enterprise, one we have built through prayer and sweat, making lots of mistakes, learning along the way, while following God into a vision greater than we could have imagined. In this book we share our continuing journey so you can discover along with us how to unleash all the resources God has given his people to enlarge his Kingdom while we live out the biblical concept of serving him every day, in all we do.

We'll begin with two guys from different mind-sets, walking unknowingly toward each other, just before their God-directed collision. Chuck Proudfit is the peanut-butter guy, living in the sticky, mental-muscle-building world of business. After earning a Harvard business degree, he moved up quickly in several large corporations. But one evening looking out over the Ohio River from the deck of his Cincinnati home, he contemplated the promotion he was about to receive from a multi-million dollar company. The career he had prepared for all his life had come down to reducing the number of sheets of toilet paper on a roll by fluffing it up. "Is this what my career is about?" he asked himself. "Is this what my *life* is to be about?"

Chuck began a ten-year spiritual journey, studying original-source texts of the world's major philosophies and religions. In the end, it was the gospel of Jesus Christ that touched Chuck's mind and heart, and he was so convinced that Christianity is true that he had to reinvent his life—his *entire* life— around it.

Eager to express his new faith in his work life, he met discouragement. The common caution, from contractors to clients, was that he shouldn't talk about religion and politics at work. When he founded SKILLSOURCE®, a business-consulting company, he hoped the new opportunities for self-direction would help him bridge the chasm between work and faith. He wanted the enterprise to honor God, but what would that look like? Sunday sermons were typically not very relevant to work life; the bookstore offered little on faith life at work; and he couldn't find an experienced Christian marketplace mentor.

Chuck and his career grew through trial and error, with inspiration from the book of Acts, where the early church seamlessly integrated faith and work. He came to realize that, as a Christian, he had to be *in* the marketplace but not *of* the marketplace. Business courses had taught him that the purpose of business is to maximize profitability or shareholder value; God was teaching him that the purpose of business is to serve others to God's glory. Chuck believed it must be possible to fulfill both goals without compromise, creating an enterprise that was Christ-centered and thrived under the best business practices.

As he led Skillsource, Chuck began applying biblical principles as a way to honor God and better develop his company and its clients. God blessed the endeavor, and Skillsource grew rapidly. In just a few short years, the firm developed a strong reputation for results, and a national base of business. Clients sought out Skillsource for its ability to deliver sustainable growth in sales, profits and people.

Seeing the blessings of applying faith principles in the marketplace, Chuck then began to bring best business practices to ministry. Stepping beyond traditional Skillsource projects, he assisted a range of local ministries to improve their infrastructure in core areas like facilities, finances, technology and human resources. By undertaking these projects, Chuck quickly learned that ministries are in huge need of marketplace talent, but are generally ambivalent about embracing it. Chuck had to learn to speak in terms comfortable to ministry, and advise action fitting to ministry's purpose and methods.

Meanwhile, as Chuck's consulting business took him to a variety of workplaces, he began seeing the daily struggles of the marketplace through spiritual eyes. He saw workplace Christians behaving no differently than non-Christian colleagues. He saw them settling for unfulfilling careers, even when they knew God was calling them to something more; compromising ethics rather than standing firm for the right thing; looking out for themselves rather than reaching out to help others succeed; and pocketing profits for a few rather than sharing resources for a greater good.

His passion ignited, Chuck became convinced that God was calling him to a career as a missionary to the marketplace. He also was headed for a collision.

Jeff Greer is the chocolate guy, living in the "sacred" world of ministry. Jeff was a youth pastor when he began to work with children living in extreme poverty. He had grown up poor in a one-bedroom apartment in New York with his mom, but that did not prepare him for what God had in store. He and his wife, Debbie, had spent the last few years renovating houses for Cincinnati families in need when they met Pat. As a single mom living in a poverty-stricken section of the city, Pat was looking for an opportunity to change the life of her family. Pat was asking for a hand up, not a handout.

Jeff and Debbie saw the poverty and hopelessness of the people in the community. They looked into the hurting, often empty eyes of the children and wanted to make a real, lasting difference. They wanted to create a sustainable solution for Pat. As they talked, Pat shared her dream to help the families in her community by providing a safe, loving environment for the children while the parents were at work.

Jeff and Debbie got together with the students in their youth ministry and decided to take on the daunting task of starting a day care center in one of the most dangerous sections of Cincinnati. The success of their efforts ignited passion in Jeff—a passion that grew as he met more children in poverty.

During a mission trip in Mexico, Jeff and a group of students and adult volunteers served a simple meal to orphans who had not eaten meat in over a year. The image of children hiding hamburgers under their beds and stuffing cookies down their pants still haunts him today. These were children without hope, unable to dream of the future. Created in the image of God, created for a purpose, they were simply existing—and that, just barely.

The following year, two of the adult leaders from that trip moved to Mexico and began to invest in the lives of at-risk children. Days after those new missionaries landed in Mexico, Jeff showed up with a group of 45 students. As he worked alongside the students, he heard a consistent theme: "I wish my mom and dad were here. They would be able to help." Their comments sparked a new vision. Jeff and the team believed if the ministry could buy land and build a facility that would allow more people to come to Mexico, a consistent flow of income could be created to support the ongoing missions work to the children. Little did Jeff know that God had already been working in the life of a local pastor. With his help, and the generosity of some ministry-minded people, Back2Back Ministries was able to purchase an old manufacturing facility in Monterrey and launch the dream into reality. Today, the ministry has grown beyond anything Jeff or the other leaders could have asked or imagined. Lives continue to be changed for the hundreds of people each year serving on Back2Back-sponsored short-term mission trips, and the ministry receives about $1.25 in donations for every dollar spent by individuals to pay for their trips.

Jeff's passion for the needy grew as he helped lead a medical team in Jos, Nigeria a few years later. As the group ministered in the Kisayip village, they were approached by a mother carrying her four-year-old son.

Weighing less than thirty pounds, his long, thin body lay limp in her arms, his mouth hanging open, his eyes lifeless. Jeff had never seen a child that close to death. His compassion for the young mother and her gaunt, emaciated child fueled his anger over their circumstances. Believing that each of us is designed by God to live an abundant life and dream of a limitless future, Jeff refused to accept that some people were meant to live without hope.

Jeff believes the responsibility to change circumstances like those he encountered in Cincinnati, Mexico and Nigeria lies squarely on the body of Christ. God instructs us in Isaiah:

> Is not this the kind of fasting I have chosen:
> to loose the chains of injustice
>   and untie the cords of the yoke,
> to set the oppressed free and break every yoke?
> Is it not to share your food with the hungry
>   and to provide the poor wanderer with shelter—
> when you see the naked, to clothe him,
>   and not to turn away from your own flesh and
> blood?[2]

God would not tell us to meet the needs of the poor without giving us the means to do it, a principle Andrew understood when by faith he brought a little boy's lunch to Jesus so he could feed more than five thousand people. He knew if Jesus gave the command, he would provide the means.

After years as a youth pastor, and then starting a new church as a senior pastor, Jeff had experienced all the traditional means of funding ministry: capital campaigns, fundraising projects, special offerings, business and community donations. Although these resources have provided for a significant amount of ministry, the budget frequently doesn't match the extent of the ministry's vision. If God gives us an epic vision, why would we beg for crumbs to try to accomplish it? If God has enlisted us in a war that cannot be won using only traditional means, we must embrace out-of-the-box solutions.

Successful, ongoing ministry needs a reliable, continuous source of funds. The problems of the world are so immense we must use every weapon God provides, looking beyond the rusty toolbox of the familiar and throwing open the armory of the unorthodox. But that's nothing new for God's people, Jeff points out: think of Gideon and his battle with the Midianites, Joshua and the battle of Jericho, David and his battle with Goliath. Unorthodox battles take an unorthodox faith, and unorthodox strategies are our Christian heritage.

Jeff envisioned a body of believers that welcomed innovation and actively sought and followed God's leading, wherever it might take them. The result was

Grace Chapel in Mason, Ohio, a church dedicated to being a global community of Christ followers awakening imagination, igniting passion and unleashing purpose.

Born of this same vision, Jeff and his wife Debbie founded Self Sustaining Enterprises (SSE) just a couple of years after the church's launch. Later, with the help of an entrepreneurial pastor from Nigeria, they co-founded SSE Nigeria. SSE, an independent organization, creates self-sustaining initiatives to eliminate pockets of poverty around the world. As president of this nonprofit, Jeff found himself in an unfamiliar world of business commitments and financial obligations very different from those in ministry. Jeff was walking in peanut butter, and it wasn't easy. He needed help.

Understanding from the parable of the talents in Matthew 25 that God has given each of us gifts and abilities that are to be used to his service, Jeff found what he was looking for right in his own congregation. God had provided a wealth of business skills and experience to the people in Jeff's own church family. One of those people was Chuck Proudfit.

Chuck and his family had just begun attending Grace Chapel when one of Jeff's Sunday messages gave new structure to Chuck's quest to integrate business and ministry. Building on the foundation of the Great Commandment (love God; love others) and the Great Commission (go into all the world and make disciples)[3],

Jeff explained how God calls all Christians to a life of purpose, a life that serves God in whatever we do. With his passion ignited and his purpose unleashed, Chuck assembled a team of researchers who spent two years helping him develop a foundation for how to live this purposeful life through work.

The result was At Work On Purpose, a non-profit organization dedicated to bringing God's guidance to the work world by helping Christians successfully live out faith at work in practical ways. Launched in Cincinnati in 2003, the ministry has grown to be the largest city-wide marketplace ministry in the U.S., serving thousands of working Christians around the world.

During planning sessions for At Work on Purpose, Chuck had coined the term "Biznistry" to refer to a faith-based business that generates profits for ministry. His initial goal was to turn Skillsource into a Biznistry that would always operate using biblical principles, and invest ALL of its profits to continue development of At Work on Purpose. Knowing that the financial requirements for At Work on Purpose would increase significantly with time, Chuck began envisioning a day when other business owners would contribute by converting their businesses into Biznistries, or even launching new enterprises that would be Biznistries from the beginning.

One day Jeff Greer and Chuck Proudfit decided to meet together and compare notes—and bam! Peanut butter and chocolate collided, and the men discovered an amazing opportunity to work together for a faster and bigger Kingdom impact. They both saw Self Sustaining Enterprises as a perfect environment for Biznistry development, and the multi-building facility of Grace Chapel—a former manufacturing plant—as a perfect venue for a Biznistry campus.

Along with many other teammates, they explored a range of options, and agreed that the Biznistries themselves would become tenants on the Grace Chapel campus. Inspired by but operating independently of the church, some of the Biznistries would be run by individual entrepreneurs. Others would be divisions of Self Sustaining Enterprises, a separate entity from the church with its own budget, board of directors and staff. SSE runs the daily operations of these businesses, using the profits generated to impact the lives of those in need.

To help coordinate the whole process, Chuck would serve as CEO of SSE, in addition to leading Skillsource and At Work on Purpose. The campus, truly a labor of love, is a testament to the premise of sustainable ministry funding, and the promise of marketplace ministry synergy.

Some Christians will be more upset that we're talking about business in a Christian context than they are that over 14 million children have lost one or both parents to AIDS in sub-Saharan Africa alone; that each day children are sold into sexual slavery, condemned to live in misery and suffering without hope. What drives Biznistry is a passion to see the least, the last, and the lost living an abundant life, a passion to see others come into a relationship with Christ, a passion to see men and women living out their purpose at work.

We strongly believe that churches must take a more active role in the challenges our world faces. The body of Christ must stop abdicating its God-given responsibility to the government or, worse, to the United Nations. If we as a church or Christian organization need to wrestle through some of the implications of moving beyond the traditional missions model, then let's do it, because the cost of following the same rutted path will be measured in lives. If you share our passion, then please read on.

The best thing about Biznistry is that it uses all the gifts and abilities of God's people and is guided by God himself. As we write this book, our desire is to challenge men and women to believe that they were created to do more than climb a ladder or build a portfolio. They were created to impact lives, using the gifts, talents and treasures that have been entrusted to them to transform others. They have been created to bring hope to a hurting world.

Our goal is to help individuals, organizations and churches stretch the boundaries of their faith. We want individuals to blur the lines between their work life and their Christian life. We want them to see their business talents as God-given gifts, to be used by him and for him. In the words of one successful businessman, "I no longer see myself as a wealth builder, but a Kingdom builder." That's the revolution we want to help move forward—men and women striving to build not their own kingdom, but God's Kingdom.

Notes

[1] <http://www.youtube.com/watch?v=gwGQ_w9lgHw>
[2] Isaiah 58:6-7
[3] Matthew 22:37; Matthew 28:18-20

1

The Great Divide

If you must see what you've never seen, you must do what you've never done. —Ed Silvoso

Bringing faith into the business world? Bringing the office to church? Is it really a good idea (or even possible) to merge these two? Integrating faith and work in today's world is generally discouraged at best, and prohibited at worst. In our experience, most Christians don't see opportunities for ministry in the marketplace. Even when we do, we rarely seize opportunities because we're afraid of being inadequate or reprimanded. This is understandable, since our relatively rare attempts are often clumsy and ineffective, unwelcome or even forbidden.

Churches and ministries are in huge need of marketplace talent, but are generally reluctant to seek it. To many in ministry, the marketplace is a "worldly" environment polluted with compromise and corruption, and filled with unfamiliar terms and approaches.

Meanwhile, the marketplace at large tends to view ministry as volunteer work performed over the weekends and inside church walls. It usually steers away from even discussing the "inflammatory" topics of religion and politics. It tends to partition church and work in formal policy, written law and unstated expectation.

The hard truth is that the work world is generally hostile to living out faith at work, and the church discourages or neglects the marketplace gifts and talents of its body. A hefty brick wall separates the two worlds in which most of us live. Sure, there's a door, but you've got to go through security. Check your faith at the door as you enter the business world, and lock your business expertise in your desk before you leave the office. No wonder we feel uncomfortable if we think of trying to integrate our work and our faith; it's like trying to sneak through security. Some of us who are more adventurous may try to straddle the wall, dangling a foot in each world. But you can't survive long on top of a wall.

We figure there's not much we can do to change the situation, assuming the wall has always been there. But brick walls aren't created by God; they're built by people, one layer at a time. This one started way back with the beginning of Western civilization, and society has slapped on more bricks and mortar to compartmentalize most facets of our lives, including church and work. To better understand how we built this wall, let's become cultural archaeologists for a while and dig down to the foundations.

Greek Bricks

In the ancient Hebrew world, the world of the Bible, life was seen as an integrated whole; there was no distinction between the sacred and the secular. God created the world and everything in it, and "saw that it was very good."[1] The world was created for God's glory.[2] Evangelical scholar George Eldon Ladd points out, "the Hebrews had no concept of nature; to them the world was the scene of God's constant activity. Thunder was the voice of God (Ps. 29:3, 5); pestilence was the heavy hand of the Lord (I Sam. 5:6); human life is the breath of God inbreathed in man's face (Gen. 2:7; Ps. 104:29)."[3] The apostle Paul also tells us that God's "invisible attributes, his eternal power and divine nature" have been "clearly seen" through all the things he made.[4] God is present in his creation, and he meant for us to encounter him and understand him through the material world.

Western culture, however, is not based on the Hebrew worldview, but on the Greek philosophy of *dualism*. Greeks believed there are two worlds—the seen and the unseen, the natural and the spiritual. The visible world is unstable, in constant change, and has only the appearance of reality.

The unseen world is the world of permanence and ultimate reality.

Dualism applied to man, too. His soul belongs to the spiritual world, and his body to the natural world. The body is nothing but a hindrance to the soul, and a wise man will learn to subdue the passions of the body and cultivate the soul. "In sum," writes Ladd, "the Greek view is that 'God' can be known only by the flight of the soul from the world and history; the Hebrew view is that God can be known because he invades history to meet men in historical experience."[5]

From the philosophy of dualism naturally followed the belief that work associated with man's spirit is the only work that has real significance. It is this belief that built the wall of separation between faith and work, leaving people in today's marketplace feeling unfulfilled and insignificant in God's Kingdom.

But this wall stands on the ideas of men, not on the foundation of God. In God's economy, *there is no sacred vs. secular; there is only sacred vs. sinful.* Everything in heaven and earth belongs to God, and we either use the resources of the material world to glorify him or to sin against him. This is true of our work just as it is every part of our life.

The Biblical Blueprint

Throughout the Bible, the action we read about is happening *at work*, and the settings are more often the marketplace than the temple. Daniel today would be a diplomat; Esther, a first lady; Lydia, a textiles buyer for a designer label; Job, a rancher; Matthew, an IRS worker; Luke, a GP physician; Tabitha, a seamstress for a non-profit. Paul, Priscilla and Aquila were tentmakers; today, perhaps sporting goods manufacturers. Many were respected political leaders: Joseph, Secretary of Agriculture; David and Solomon, heads of state; Deborah, a judge. The "noble wife" of Proverbs 31 was the original working mother, caring for her family and helping the needy while planting a vineyard, buying land, making cloth, and selling it in the market. Stories of the faith of these Bible heroes and heroines happen in their *working world*. We have become so accustomed to the work/faith divide that when we read the Bible, we miss this.

There is nothing "secular" about work in the Bible. The Hebrew verb *avad* is used in the Old Testament for both "work" and "worship." It is related to our word vocation, which even today is defined first in the Oxford English Dictionary as "the action on the part of God, calling a person to exercise some special function, especially for a spiritual nature or to fill a certain position." How sad it is that we usually live out a later definition for vocation: it's only a job. The word work in its different forms is used more than 800 times in the Bible, more than all the words used to express worship, music, praise, and singing combined.[6] Clearly, God is concerned about the work we do and how and why we do it.

What would Jesus do in the marketplace? How would Jesus do ministry? We clearly see his example in the Bible. He didn't sit in the temple and say "come and see"; He modeled an active "go and be." Consider his example of integrating faith and work:

- Of Jesus' 132 public appearances in the New Testament, 122 were in the marketplace.
- Of 52 parables Jesus told, 45 had a workplace context.
- Jesus spent his adult life as a carpenter until age 30 before he went into a preaching ministry in the workplace.
- Jesus called 12 workplace individuals, not clergy, to build his church.[7]

Jesus could have called rabbis or temple officials to form his group of twelve followers, but he didn't. In fact, some of Jesus' harshest words were directed to the Pharisees and teachers of the law. Instead, Jesus chose men from the marketplace. He called Peter, Andrew, James and John from their fishing boats; Matthew came from his tax-collecting booth.

The apostle Paul, too, merged his work with his ministry. In Acts 18:2-4, we're told that Paul practiced his tent-making vocation with Priscilla and Aquila *while he ministered* in Corinth. His famous sermon in Athens, recorded in Acts 17, took place on Mars Hill "in the meeting of the Areopagus" (v. 22). The Areopagus was not a religious body, but a judicial one. Paul brought his evangelistic message right into the court's meeting place. Paul tells the Ephesian believers, "You yourselves know that these hands of mine have supplied my own needs and the needs of my companions. In everything I did, I showed you that by this kind of hard work we must help the weak."[8] Paul is a living example that it's possible, even admirable, to make tents and preach the Word, to blend business and ministry.

The first-century Christian church had no separation between faith and work. It was natural for the earliest Christ followers to pursue work spiritually, and the fruits of their efforts were supernatural. The Book of Acts records this era, during which thousands of people were brought to Christ, the apostles performed miracles, and poverty was eliminated within the emerging Christian community.[9] God was clearly at work in the first-century marketplace, for it was the scene for 39 of the 40 divine interventions recorded in Acts.[10]

Jesus is Lord not just of what we call sacred, but of the entire natural world. When God raised Jesus from the dead, he "placed all things under his feet and appointed him to be head over everything for the church, which is his body, the fullness of him who fills everything in every way."[11] Jesus is head over *everything*—our families, our local church, our community, our work. If we chop off a section of the world, set it apart and label it "secular," aren't we claiming it does not belong under Christ's lordship? Aren't we perverting biblical truth?

Being a Christian is integrating God in every part of our lives—it's who we are, not what we do. We can't park Christ on the shelf next to the Bible as we head out the door on Monday morning. Scripture tells us, *"Whatever you do, work at it with all your heart, as working for the Lord, not for men, since you know that you will receive an inheritance from the Lord as a reward. It is the Lord Christ you are serving."*[12] Think about this—we should *work* for the *Lord*, which means doing God's work while we're at work! This scripture is God's truth, and truth doesn't contradict itself. We are called to serve God, not just customers or colleagues, in our place of work.

Sadly, the biblical blueprint of integrating Christ in all aspects of our lives was crumpled a long time ago and tossed in the trash. Our churches and our culture have accepted, even encouraged, the building of an unbiblical wall between faith and work. This Great Divide casts an equally great shadow, weakening the church and leaving an enormous mission field largely ignored. Businesses grope in the dark without godly guidance, and individuals are frustrated and unfulfilled.

Living in the Wall's Shadow

Robert Adamson was one of these. Raised in a close Christian family, he studied at culinary school under one of only twelve Master Chefs in the U.S. He worked in the restaurant business for over 20 years at the Executive Chef level in some of Cincinnati's premiere restaurants, as well as running his own catering business. Although he worked long hours, he always made time outside his regular job to volunteer at soup kitchens or work in youth ministry. But he never felt it was enough. When he helped at a soup kitchen that had to enforce a time limit for diners, Robert felt frustrated that those served received only food and not the love and relationships they desperately needed.

Robert saw another whole level of ministry in his cousin, who ministers in Haiti. "I felt I had it in me," says Robert. But he wasn't convinced God was asking him to be a foreign missionary.

Clearly, God is not calling all Christians to traditional vocational ministry. Scripture tells us God gifted *some* to be apostles, prophets, evangelists, pastors, and teachers. Their purpose? *To prepare God's people for works of service.*[13] It is God's people, not just professional clergy, who are to go out and do God's work. But churches largely fail to give their people a vision for ministry that allows them to use their gifts. We have given the message that if you want to serve God, you do it through the church. Churches plead for Sunday School teachers and nursery workers, but fail to be good stewards of the abilities of electricians, lawyers, designers, health care providers, and computer engineers.

The local church tends to separate the "spiritual" from the "secular." The marketplace is seen as a "worldly" environment with funds for church growth and leaders for projects, but not as ministry in and of itself. Church members often feel their pastor doesn't relate to them, never having lived in the business world. Even worse, they may feel they are "second-class" Christians because much of their life is dedicated to work that has little to do with God.

The result is that most believers feel they are in two different worlds. Faith is not accepted in business, and business is not accepted in ministry. Somehow we've created a world where we go to church on Sundays and work on Mondays, and we don't look for ways to integrate;

we default to separate. This separation hurts both business and ministry by creating divided purpose, fractured ethics, and segregated resources.

Divided Purpose

Several years ago Lee Iacocca, the former CEO of Chrysler, was asked what advice he would give to the younger generation coming up the corporate ladder. He said he would tell them when you get to the top, there's nothing there.

The Bible, too, tells us that fame, popularity, wealth and power are all meaningless apart from God. King Solomon, one of the richest men who ever lived, tells us in Ecclesiastes, "Yet when I surveyed all that my hands had done and what I had toiled to achieve, everything was meaningless, a chasing after the wind; nothing was gained under the sun."[14]

Like Solomon, workplace Christians realize that marketplace performance without an underlying ministry purpose is ultimately meaningless. But we settle for unfulfilling careers, even when we know God is calling us to something more. God has "set eternity in the hearts of men,"[15] yet we spend most of our lives toiling in the daily grind to meet temporal needs and desires. We long to make a difference, but find we're spending all our energy just to make a dollar.

Many Christians miss feeling true fulfillment in their work because most non-church organizations lack an eternal purpose. In the day-to-day work world, we can feel disconnected from a true calling, and even disconnected from God himself. If the purpose of work is to accomplish work of purpose, how do we get there?

The key to finding real fulfillment in our work is to seek *significance* that goes beyond *success*. These two terms were popularized through Bob Buford's best-selling book *Halftime*. Buford's premise is that we often spend the first half of our work lives pursuing the world's definition of success, discovering that it is ultimately empty. For many of us, it is in mid-life that we step back to reconsider, and chart a new course. It is at this point that we shift our career objectives from "success" to "significance," to the building of God's Kingdom in the work world rather than our own or an employer's.

Generation Y already understands this, even as they are just starting their careers. They've seen the mid-life crises of their older counterparts, and they don't plan to follow the same route. Young workers want to know they are making a difference in the world, right from the start.

No matter our age, Jesus is calling us to work lives that are spiritually productive, not just materially profitable. It is by embracing significance over success that we come to understand Jesus' assurance to us in John 10:10, that he came so that his followers might have an abundant life, a life lived to the fullest. We are all called, in unique ways, to a purpose of spiritual significance in the work place.

This life of faith at work can happen anywhere—we don't have to leave our job to serve God. Christians all over the world are now responding to God's call to be a light in the marketplace, discovering as many ways to honor God through their work as there are places of business. God places many of his own in companies that don't include him in their mission statement, making them points of light in an otherwise dark place. God calls other Christians to serve him in a different way, sometimes moving them to a new place of work.

Chef Robert Adamson discovered his calling through a message at his church. As he learned how his Personality, Learnings, Abilities and Yearnings (PLAY) could be used by God for his purposes, Robert's heart and mind were opened. That's when he took a step of faith.

"I set aside my past life, a materialistic, greed-based life," Robert says.

The new life God gave him was one of relationships. Using his talent to provide healthy, affordable meals, his heart to reach out to people in need, and his experience in volunteer ministry, Robert opened a community café in a

Dayton, Ohio suburb where one in three children go to bed hungry every night. ONE ("Our Neighbors Eat") Bistro offers an open door and healthy, fresh, affordable food to all comers, regardless of ability to pay. Paying customers are encouraged to "pay it forward" to support the ministry; those who cannot pay may give their time in restaurant work in exchange for a meal. At One Bistro, the community comes together and relationships are top priority.

"We provide a hopeful, healing sanctuary environment—this is how the people we serve describe it to me," says Robert. "To be involved in building God-centered relationships is awesome. I'm blessed every day in this place." When Robert gave up society's idea of success to embrace God's plan for him, he found what was missing in his old work life.

If we believe God's Word, then it must be possible, *though not necessarily easy,* to create work environments that glorify God and enable us to help fulfill his larger purposes. God must make it possible to integrate Christian faith and work. If we believe God's Word, the bottom line is that marketplace and ministry must have the potential to be complementary rather than contradictory.

PASSION

Bringing together people in the local community, both those in need of help and those with help to give, building relationships while enjoying good food.

PURPOSE

To eliminate hunger, grow relationships, and celebrate community; to provide a hand up rather than a hand out.

PLAN

Provide healthy, affordable meals in a warm and welcoming environment, using a "pay what you can" concept. Any donations received over the suggested price to "pay it forward" will help cover the cost of a neighbor's meal. If unable to pay, neighbors can give their time in service as payment.

PRACTICE

Staff: Two chefs; all other roles filled by volunteers

Finances: Took in $250,000 the first year; of this, $70,000 was pay-it-forward money. Average "tip" is 40%, covering the cost of all free meals to those who cannot pay.

Keys to Success:

> "On the surface, everything about this enterprise says failure— but this place is thriving. We know it's all about God."
>
> Founder and Chef
> Robert Adamson

- Everyone gets a Mission Menu when they come in, explaining the pay-what-you-can concept and encouraging diners who are able to "pay it forward"
- Emphasis on relationship-building develops a sense of community and desire to help one another
- Online signup for volunteers
- Help for those in need goes beyond food to ongoing support through relationships, referrals, and even guidance for starting their own micro-enterprises

Fractured Ethics

Deceptive financial officers in handcuffs. Greedy executives lining their pockets. Sub-standard products harming consumers. The list goes on and on. Most organizations compromise biblical principles for what they call the "practical realities" of the marketplace. In every area, from ethics to stewardship, most organizations fall far short of their God-given potential. And Christians are often falling with them.

As soon as Chuck became a Christian, he began viewing the daily struggles of the marketplace through spiritual eyes. He saw workplace Christians behaving no differently than non-Christian colleagues. He saw them settling for unfulfilling careers, even when they knew God was calling them to something more; compromising ethics, rather than standing firm for the right thing; looking out for themselves, rather than reaching out to help others succeed; and pocketing profits for a few, rather than sharing resources for a greater good. We were made to "shine like stars in the universe" as we "hold out the word of life,"[16] but instead many of us tarnish in our cubicles until we blend in with the non-Christians around us.

The corporate world is starving for the influence of Christians who bring their faith—including integrity, honesty, and truth—to the marketplace. Yet faith is not accepted in business, and the church in America has isolated itself from the business world. Christians fail to accomplish God's purposes for us at work because we fail to follow his commandments in the marketplace.

As a pastor, Jeff asked himself why the church does not walk in the world where the majority of the body spends most of its time. The church talks a lot about God; it talks some about family; but it talks very, very little about the workplace. We are all "called to belong to Jesus Christ,"[17] and we don't stop belonging to him when we're in an office or a factory or a school. Yet the church has left the members of its body to fend for themselves in the workplace. The church, Jeff insists, must address the real issues Christians face at work: finding a noble work purpose, facing temptations in the workplace, and learning how God wants to use our gifts and abilities.

Generally, contemporary Christianity views the marketplace as little more than a venue for generating ministry funds for the local church. This is a tragedy that has separated most of the Christian community from most of the ministry opportunity! When Jesus commands, "Go into all the world and preach the gospel," he makes no exception for the workplace. According to researcher George Barna, only 3% of Christians are employed in vocational ministry. The other 97% are in the marketplace, oblivious that most of the workforce is unchurched and represents an enormous mission field.

Marketplace Christians spend the majority of their waking hours at work, which means that available time for ministry is at its peak in the marketplace. The typical marketplace Christian also has a "congregation"—consisting of colleagues, customers, suppliers, and the surrounding community—larger and more diverse than the average local church. Envision, then, what an impact working Christians could have if they embraced their role as missionaries to the marketplace.

Ethics go beyond simply avoiding the illegal and the immoral. Ethics for a Christian mean obedience to God—whether at home, at church, or in the work world. The Great Commission and the Great Commandment not only define our purpose, but also our conduct. When Jesus says, "Love your neighbor as yourself," he's not just talking about the guy next door, but the guy in the next office, and the guy down the street. In fact, when we can get on a plane and fly anywhere on earth in a day, my neighbor becomes anyone in need.

Many of us have lost our sensitivity and have become hardened to the spiritual need and the physical suffering in the world. Our lives have been difficult so it's been hard to focus on others, or our lives have been prosperous and we've forgotten what it was like to live without hope.

Yet scripture makes it clear that focusing on ourselves while others suffer incurs God's wrath. The biblical explanation of Sodom's destruction is a great illustration of this. If you ask Christians why Sodom was destroyed, most will say it was because of the city's sexual perversion. But that is a one-sided view of what Scripture teaches. Ezekiel records that God says an important reason he destroyed Sodom was that it refused to share with the poor:

> "Now this was the sin of your sister Sodom: She and her daughters were arrogant, overfed and unconcerned; they did not help the poor and needy. They were haughty and did detestable things before me. Therefore I did away with them as you have seen."[18]

These verses don't say that they oppressed the poor, although they may have. It accuses them of not helping those in need. God liberates the needy, and we are commanded in his Word to do the same. If we are his body, why aren't we doing everything in our power to bring hope and help to those who need it?

Although physical need in the world is more tangible, spiritual need is just as great. Not only are Christians called to care for the poor and sick, but also for those who are spiritually suffering. The book of Acts describes how many of the apostles dedicated their lives to introducing nonbelievers to Christ and helping Christians to grow in their faith. Jesus gave the Great Commission not only to them, but also to us, commanding us to go and make disciples.

God makes it clear that Christians in the work world must go beyond dealing fairly in the marketplace and not cheating on our taxes. We are to also obey his command to "Love your neighbor as yourself" by focusing on the spiritual and physical needs of others. This is a call to Christians in the work world to make a difference rather than just a dollar. It is a call to construct enterprises that provide innovative answers to how and why we conduct business so we can make a positive impact on the world.

Segregated Resources

In Bible times, the greatest material resources were locked up with the kings. But today, the greatest material resources—the money, the talent, the equipment, the facilities—are locked up in the marketplace. This means that in most local churches, there's a big gap between the vision for ministry and the financial resources available. Our vision is bigger than our budget. But with God's empowerment, the body of Christ can pick the locks, throw open the doors, and use marketplace resources to change lives around the world.

Scripture has much to say about being thrifty with money, and church leaders generally understand the theory and desire to be good stewards of God's resources. The problem comes when leaders lack the practical skills to efficiently manage and distribute these resources. Here is where the skills of God's people from the world of business can enhance the work of ministry.

In the Parable of the Talents, Jesus illustrates how God expects believers to *invest* the capital he has provided to grow his Kingdom. The servant who "put his money to work and gained five more" was praised by his master, while the servant who buried his talent and returned it to his master was called wicked and lazy.[19] This parable calls all Christians to go beyond the status quo, by seeking effective strategies to invest money, time, and talent in the growth of God's Kingdom.

It is no coincidence that the Parable of the Talents is followed in Scripture by the metaphor of the Sheep and the Goats. Jesus teaches us that resources aren't to be buried, but rather to be invested for a return. Then he shows us the *purpose* for this investment: we are to reach beyond ourselves to help those in desperate need. The physical act of mobilizing all our resources to serve others is what demonstrates our love for God and the righteousness we have received through Jesus Christ.

Considering the overwhelming need in the world, churches need to go beyond donations and other traditional measures to create innovative solutions to fight physical and spiritual poverty. We need a strategy that takes on a life of its own, continuing to exist far beyond the individual donor. We must create long-term sustainability in pockets of poverty and where there is spiritual need.

To accomplish this, we need more than just money. The resources God provides his people include our minds, our gifts, our abilities, and our experiences, as well as what's in our wallets. It is going to take the whole body of Christ, with all of our varied resources, working together to further the cause of Christ.

As a youth pastor for fifteen years, Jeff watched young people agonize over the choice of going into the ministry or going into the marketplace. "You know, I really want to go into ministry," they would tell him, "but I have these abilities and these gifts for business, and I don't know which way to go." They almost felt like they were selling out if they went to the marketplace. But many of the gifts God gives us can be used in business as well as in the church. Jeff believes it's his job as a pastor to equip church members to use *all* their gifts, abilities, and experiences to do God's work, wherever that may be.

Just as Christ's body has all the resources needed to accomplish its ministry, it also has everything necessary to be successful in the business arena. Jeff has learned as a senior pastor to see the body of Christ as his greatest resource for successful ministry in both the church and the marketplace. When he asks people what they do for a living, he is asking that for a specific purpose: to better understand how God may use them. "By asking this question," says Jeff, "I get a lot of really gifted people involved in different areas of ministry, many of which go beyond the traditional boundaries of 'church.'"

Often pastors have lamented the fact that few men are active in the ministries of their church. Jeff's broader view of ministry has allowed him to recruit men at Grace Chapel not just to positions as small group leaders and Sunday school teachers, but also to serve in administration, finance, landscaping, accounting, trade work, sports ministry, marketing, and in the development of Biznistries. Since the body of Christ is battling for the lives of people, we need to draft everyone available to insure victory. Church members must be given direction, encouragement, and permission to use *all* their gifts and talents in God's service. Biznistry provides new opportunities to do just that.

Tearing Down the Wall

We've seen how the brick wall between church and work in today's world discourages and even prevents both individuals and organizations from fulfilling God's purposes. Faith is not accepted in business, and business is not accepted in ministry. Scripture tells us it is not only possible, but also necessary, to tear down the wall between faith and work. Marketplace and ministry can be complementary rather than contradictory.

So how will we accomplish what God has called us to do? Throughout biblical history, God has instructed his people during critical times to use unique and unorthodox battle plans. And certainly the need has never been more critical. Just as in Joshua's time, God will tear down walls for his people. All of us can pursue ministry in the marketplace wherever we have influence. Our impact can be everything from a kind word, to a better-developed employee, to the creation of a new organization with a God-honoring purpose.

It's beginning to happen. Christians throughout the world are starting to cross man-made boundaries to carry their faith into the work world. Whether expressed as Faith at Work, Christian Entrepreneurship, or Business as Mission, this movement of God in the 21st century is perhaps the greatest revival in the body of Christ in modern times.

Imagine a new enterprise built from the ground up to honor God at every level—a new kind of organization, with a Christ-centered work environment, right in the midst of the general marketplace. Imagine the rebirth of an existing enterprise, transformed at the organizational level by placing God at the center of an integrated faith/work system. Imagine creating an *integrated synergy* between business and ministry.

There is a way to do this, and there is a name for it... Biznistry.

Notes

[1] Genesis 1:31

[2] Psalms 19:1

[3] George Eldon Ladd, *The Pattern of New Testament Truth*, pp. 13-40. 1968. Wm. B. Eerdmans Publishing. Reprinted in *Present Truth Magazine*, <http://www.presenttruthmag.com/archive/XXIX/29-2.htm>

[4] Romans 1:20

[5] Ladd, *op. cit.*

[6] Os Hillman, "Changing the 80/20 Rule in the 9 to 5 Window," *In the Workplace.* <http://www.intheworkplace.com/apps/articles/default.asp?articleid=12865&columnid=1935>

[7] *Ibid.*

[8] Acts 20:34-5

[9] Acts 2:42-47

[10] Hillman, *op. cit.*

[11] Ephesians 1:22

[12] Colossians 3:23-24

[13] Ephesians 4:11-12

[14] Ecclesiastes 2:11

[15] Ecclesiastes 3:11

[16] Philippians 2:16

[17] Romans 1:6

[18] Ezekiel 16:49-50

[19] Matthew 25:14-30

2

Why Biznistry?

A man has made at least a start on discovering the meaning of human life when he plants shade trees under which he knows full well he will never sit. —D. Elton Trueblood

Jerry pulled off his baseball cap and playfully plopped it on the head of the little girl sitting on the low stone wall beside him. "It's yours," he said. Femi didn't know English, but she understood. She threw her arms around his neck and he squeezed her tight as his daughter Jenna snapped their picture. He would miss her.

Early tomorrow morning he'd be leaving Africa after a week-long mission trip that had changed his life. Sure, it had been hot, and dust got into everything, including the food. But here he discovered he could help change lives. Jenna, Jerry's youngest of three children, had been excited when her high school youth group planned the trip, and Jerry had reluctantly agreed to serve as a chaperone. Each day of the week had been packed with distributing medical supplies and clothing they had brought with them, pouring cement for a schoolhouse, and playing with the children at Femi's orphanage. The orphanage had no running water, and most of the older kids spent a good part of their day hauling water from another village rather than going to school.

The people needed so much—clean water, education, jobs, health care. Jerry admired the missionaries who worked all year long with these impoverished people, sacrificing their own comfort so others could live better and learn to love the Lord. It was worth it, he decided, to give up some creature comforts in order to have a sense of purpose and real significance in your life.

But Jerry had a family and a job waiting for him back home, back in the "real world." Jerry loved his family, loved his God, and tolerated his work (on the good days). Somebody had to bring in the cash; college and food and mission trips didn't pay for themselves. Jerry had worked his way up through several positions in marketing to eventually become a brand manager for a large manufacturer of kitchen goods. He'd been excited in his first job, designing creative ad copy and seeing it in print.

But after twenty-five years in the field, Jerry had a hard time convincing himself his efforts to sell more casserole dishes made any real difference in the world. He wanted to serve God, and did what he could. He was close to giving a full tithe to the church; at least his work made that possible. When his church added on to the building, Jerry was able to get a bunch of supplies for the new kitchen at a greatly reduced cost from his company. He and his wife worked in the nursery once a month, and chaperoning on this trip certainly helped out the youth group. But wasn't there something more? He longed to feel he was being used of God, every day. How could he go back to promoting a new flowery design on a microwave dish when these kids in Africa didn't even have clean water to drink?

Seizing Significance

Jerry is fictional, but his story is real. He represents an ever-increasing number of Christians who long for meaningful work that is more than just a job.

For some, it's not until after years of striving for a successful work life, moving up the pay scale, that we begin to wonder if what we're achieving, or trying to achieve, is true success. For Chuck Proudfit, the longing for something more came in his twenties:

"As I graduated from Harvard, I envisioned what work would be like—to be part of a fast track, employed at a training ground, to make my mark, to leave a legacy, to climb the corporate ladder. Then after only a few years in the marketplace, that's exactly what I was doing. But I didn't like where it was leading, and I didn't know what to replace it with.

"One evening I sat out on my balcony overlooking the Ohio River. Unlike Colorado's clear creeks and streams where I grew up, this river looked more like a mass of mud. It was moving slowly downhill, and that's how my career felt to me.

"Looking for a deeper significance for my life, I embarked on a ten-year spiritual journey that culminated in dedicating my life to Jesus Christ. He became the source of my personal significance. But how was I to live a life of significance for God while at work? I seemed to run into a brick wall every way I turned."

We've already had a look at that brick wall. God created each of us for a special purpose in his Kingdom, and it is only when we discover and live out that purpose for something beyond ourselves that we experience fulfillment and significance. So the first reason for considering Biznistry is to create purpose-filled, meaningful work in the business world that advances the Kingdom of God. Biznistries provide a platform for ministry to all in their sphere of influence—employees, clients, community, competitors, and the mission work they support.

PASSION

To unleash dreams, resource opportunities, and transform lives while strategically eliminating poverty all over the world.

PURPOSE

To generate start-up funds for building self-sustaining enterprises in global pockets of poverty, to serve the local community by providing employment, affordable goods, and funding for Back2Back and other ministries.

PLAN

Resell donated, quality merchandise at bargain prices in thrift stores run by Self-Sustaining Enterprises, a 501(c)(3) organization based in Mason, Ohio

PRACTICE

Staff: Director of stores, full- and part-time paid staff, volunteers

> "Serving locally; giving globally. Our proceeds bless those who have the least and need the most."

Finances: Former warehouse building on the Grace Chapel campus was renovated largely by volunteers; store furnishings bought at bargain prices from stores gone out of business; merchandise is donated, so start-up costs were minimal.

Keys to Success:

- Well-lighted store with wide aisles, fitting rooms, and friendly staff to create a pleasant shopping experience
- Quick turnover of goods, bargain prices, and many sale events so customers keep coming back
- Friendly staff, Christian music, referrals for social services and prayer request notebook at the checkout to demonstrate God's love to customers
- Marketing in a variety of outlets, including social media and conventions

Planning for Provision

To understand a second reason for considering Biznistry, let's get back to Jerry. He was pensive as the plane took off the next morning, headed toward home. He kept thinking of Femi and the other children at the orphanage. He had known for a long time there were many in the world who lived in such poor conditions—but meeting them and interacting with them had suddenly brought them into his own sphere. Certainly, God considered them among the "neighbors" he was to love. But what could Jerry do, once he was home, to make a difference in their lives?

His daughter, too, wanted to continue to help. "Our youth group could have a second-hand clothes drive, and send the clothes to the kids," Jenna suggested. Jerry admired her enthusiasm, but knew her idea was impractical; who would pay for shipping? Jenna suggested a car wash every week to raise money. But what these kids needed were clean water and teachers, not just T-shirts and a few bucks. Surely the church as a whole would respond when they heard of the need, he thought. Some would be moved to give; maybe they could even raise enough to hire someone to dig a well. Wait—maybe the church could buy well-digging equipment and start a well-digging business, giving jobs to needy African men who would travel from village to village, digging wells! It would even be an opportunity to spread the gospel. Think of the lives that would be changed!

Jerry's excitement quickly faded. He knew the church was looking to hire a new children's director, and was currently scraping up funds for some needed electrical work in their building. Two men and a single mom in the church had lost their jobs in the recent bad economy, and the church was helping their families. Even if people were generous, there were so many needs and only so much the people could give. Why would God continue to bring needs to the church's doorstep, and not supply the resources to meet them?

The dilemma Jerry faced is common in the body of Christ: our vision is bigger than our budget. The greatest material resources—the money, the talent, the equipment, the facilities—are in the marketplace. This means that in most local churches, there's a big gap between the vision for ministry and the financial resources available.

For years the church and other organizations have attacked the problem of poverty, education, nutrition and healthcare from one general perspective: asking donors for money. This strategy depends mostly on the financial position and interest of those participating, which makes it limited in its scope and inconsistent in its implementation. We become accustomed to taking in crumbs and giving them out, then hoping for more crumbs.

Competition for donated dollars is intense. Over two million nonprofits operate in the United States, and from 2000 to 2010 the number of public charities registered with the IRS, including religious groups, rose 24%.[1] Tight economic times and recent high unemployment have caused many people to decrease their giving, meaning donations are spread even more thinly over an ever-increasing number of organizations.

Imagine how much better it would be to create something that continues to exist far beyond the individual donor. And instead of expecting individuals to give just their finances, what if they gave their minds, their gifts, their abilities and their experiences to change lives wherever there is physical, spiritual, or any other need?

Biznistry is just such a strategy. In the pages that follow, we'll look deeper into the reasons to consider this unconventional approach to performing ministry in the business world, and illustrate through examples how a Biznistry functions. As they say in TV prescription drug ads, Biznistry is not for everyone. It requires patience, skill, resources, and dedication. But with God's empowerment, the body of Christ can use market resources to change lives and advance the Kingdom of God while performing meaningful, fulfilling work in the business world. This is what Biznistry is all about.

Notes

[1] A. Blackwood, K. Roeger, and S. Pettijohn, *The Nonprofit Sector in Brief, 2012*. Urban Institute. <http://www.urban.org/UploadedPDF/412674-The-Nonprofit-Sector-in-Brief.pdf

3

What is Biznistry?

The Christian ideal has not been tried and found wanting. It has been found difficult and left untried. – G.K. Chesterton

The sun was just coming up as Jerry backed down his driveway to go to work, being careful to avoid the two trash cans near the curb awaiting the garbage truck. His headlights swept across the yard as he turned into the street, and then shone on a young woman at the end of his neighbor's driveway. Jerry slowly rolled past as she hefted a set of metal shelves into the back of her pickup truck—shelves that looked a bit swayed and needing paint, apparently hauled out for the garbage truck and destined for the landfill. Jerry wondered about the woman who had come out early to drive the dark streets looking at other people's trash. He also thought his neighbor would be happy to know this woman had found a new purpose for them.

It wasn't the first time he'd seen one person's trash become someone else's treasure. When Jenna was about six or seven, his wife Sarah had rescued a child's old wooden puppet stage from the curb and she and Jenna had had fun painting it and hanging some fabric for a curtain. The stage had sparked Jenna's creativity, and her puppet shows had entertained the family all that next year. What the community needed, Jerry decided, was a central place to gather reusable "junk" where others could see it with new eyes. Customers would even be willing to pay, happy to get some real bargains.

Jerry's mind for business and marketing, together with his deep desire to help the children he had met in Africa, sorted out possibilities throughout his drive to work that morning. By the time he parked his car, he was bursting with a vision that filled him with energy and excitement. He pictured a tidy second-hand store, stocked with bargains donated by people in his church and town, *purposed from the beginning* to raise funds for a well-digging crew in Africa. It would require time, of course, and some shrewd planning, but once established, the store would be a self-sustaining source of revenue for a small business overseas dedicated to bringing clean water to those who needed it most. The store wouldn't only help people overseas; it would also serve Jerry's local community by providing items at rock-bottom prices for customers hit hard by the poor economy, and even jobs for people like those in his church who were out of work. The store could minister to people like the woman he had seen on the street that morning, touching them with the love of Jesus Christ. Jerry envisioned a new kind of enterprise that combined a heart for ministry with the best practices of business, a place that brought real, God-serving purpose to daily work.

Jerry and many others like him, searching for a way to make a real difference in the world with their work, have challenged the norm and blurred the cultural boundary between faith and work. Some of these pioneers have never heard the term Biznistry, but we have found the term helpful in describing a specific kind of work that embraces the best of both business and ministry.

A Biznistry is a self-sustaining enterprise commissioned for a Kingdom purpose, operating according to biblical principles, integrating ministry at every level, and releasing a flow of funds for further ministry advances.

Biznistries blend the best of marketplace and ministry disciplines wherever they meet needs in the world. The need may be physical, emotional, or spiritual in nature, or any combination of these. Biznistries generate profits in a lucrative area of the marketplace to create investment capital that funds these needs. Biznistries are formed intentionally for the purpose of glorifying and serving God, by workplace Christians who focus on improving the world rather than impressing the world.

Financially, a Biznistry delivers profits like a business, but distributes profits like a ministry. It pursues a strong profit opportunity, using biblical principles, to create a sustainable flow of investment capital. It reinvests as many profit dollars as possible toward addressing the pressing need defined in its purpose.

Everyone can appreciate the attraction of a way to raise funds for philanthropy, but there is more to Biznistry than finances. Just as Christians have a worldview that is set apart from the norm, Biznistries reflect a "work view" that is set apart from the norm. Because their leaders must answer to God, Biznistries insist on following the highest standards of biblical conduct. From a ministry perspective, these include sharing the Gospel and helping the hurting. From a business perspective, these standards include sustained profitability and continual improvement. Biznistries are as passionate about growing people as growing profits, and success is measured not simply by funds raised, but also by lives touched.

Spiritually, a Biznistry is a place of worship, because Christians are called to glorify God in *all* they do. It is a place for ministry, where people are a first priority. It is a place for evangelism, because Biznistry workers are God's ambassadors in the work world. It is a place offering fellowship, as leaders and employees work together toward a common vision and purpose. It is a place coordinating discipleship, for it recognizes that spiritual growth produces wisdom and faithfulness.

"A cord of three strands is not easily broken." So Solomon tells us in Ecclesiastes 4:12. In the same way, marketplace and ministry are strongest when they are intertwined with each other, and around God. This view is in marked contrast to the prevailing philosophies today: *isolationism*, in which marketplace and ministry are separated; or *minimalism*, in which the marketplace makes ministry as invisible as possible and ministry makes the marketplace as invisible as possible. The "three-strand cord" philosophy is one of *synergism* between marketplace and ministry, centered on God.

Biznistry boils down to ministry in and through business. It requires us to view business not as just a contributor to the church, but as an extension of the church; to put aside business as usual, and practice business in service to ministry. By demolishing the wall between business and ministry, Biznistries can go more places and impact more lives than either component can separately.

Biznistry vs. Organizational Alternatives

Biznistries are just one kind of organization, and are best understood relative to the alternatives. The following graphic compares Biznistry to three general categories we will call Basic Business, Better Business, and Charity. The horizontal axis measures application of best business practices, from lower to higher. The vertical axis measures application of best ministry practices, from lower to higher.

Biznistry vs. Organizational Alternatives

Basic Businesses fall short both in good business practices and in good ministry practices. They focus single-mindedly on maximum profits in minimum time. They have little regard for anyone or anything hurt in the process. Basic Businesses are usually quick to come and go; in our generation, examples include pyramid schemes, Internet spam, and pornography shops.

Unlike a Basic Business, a Charity has a strong ministry emphasis. Created to serve the needy, it has a purpose similar to that of a Biznistry. However, a Charity has less business emphasis. For example, a charity must continually seek donor funding to maintain operations, but a Biznistry establishes a sustainable flow of funds from profitable business activity.

Like a Biznistry, a Better Business has a strong business emphasis, seeking sustainability and growth while developing its employees. Ministry practices in a Better Business, however, are secondary. Most Better Businesses make charitable contributions, but a Biznistry targets 100% of its available profits for ministry. Social Enterprises may be considered Better Businesses with an even stronger focus on philanthropy; we'll discuss how they differ from Biznistry at the end of this chapter.

Where they're led by faithful, practicing Christians, we find that Charities, Better Businesses, and Biznistries are ALL honorable efforts because they are biblically operated. Only the Basic Business consistently falls short of biblical standards. Let's be clear: God calls deeply committed Christians to serve throughout the marketplace, and he equips believers differently according to his purposes. Biznistry is just one kind of organization that will be a good fit for some. A closer look at the distinctive traits that all

Biznistries share will give you a better idea if Biznistry is right for you.

Self-Sustaining

While charities fund their activities primarily with donations, Biznistries fund ministry with their own business profits, providing a regular, reliable source of support for their target projects. Those planning a Biznistry, just as traditional entrepreneurs, must examine the marketplace to determine if their business idea is economically feasible. Our Aquaponics venture, for example, was in a trial phase for several years. Combining a fish farm with hydroponically-grown vegetables nourished by the fish waste showed promise for providing a year-round source of protein and fresh produce, as well as jobs, for villages in Nigeria. But if the enterprise could not turn a profit, it would not be a Biznistry.

Of course, any business startup, including a Biznistry, needs initial funding and time to become profitable— typically several years. Careful monitoring during this early phase will help determine if the enterprise promises future profitability. Our original New2You thrift store is now generating profits for overseas and local ministry, but we closed another branch because it was not profitable, probably due to its location. Similarly, we may find that the Aquaponics enterprise is a viable Biznistry in Nigeria, but does not function the same way in the U.S. As our experience in Aquaponics grows, we have been able to use the system to inspire, educate, and motivate, but not yet to turn a profit.

This does not mean that an enterprise that cannot sustain itself is worthless. Our Aquaponics experience in the U.S. currently serves an educational function—to promote farming Biznistries overseas—rather than a profit-making function. Other kinds of ventures may be worthwhile for other reasons. One of the New2You thrift stores, for example, is run independently by a Cincinnati church. After several years, the church must still contribute funds to keep it running. The store, however, has created jobs in a depressed area, its ministry has brought dozens of people to Christ, and it serves as an example of Christian business principles. In fact, it has been so successful in ministering to the community that the church has decided to continue it. An enterprise may be worthy because it meets needs even if it is not financially profitable; however, we would call this a ministry rather than a Biznistry.

The disadvantaged people served by Biznistry are blessed because the support they receive is sustainable. Orphans, for example, can receive financial support throughout their childhood, not just for a week here or there. Self Sustaining Enterprises, Inc., supported in part by the New2You thrift store and other Biznistries, is making a remarkable impact on the needy in Jos, Nigeria. Take, for example, a group of twelve widows, most with children to support, who lost their husbands to AIDS. While providing the women a business plan and guidance, SSE purchased a $1,200 water pump for the group. The equipment allowed the women to irrigate a much larger agricultural plot than would be possible with the usual method of irrigation, toting one bucket at a time from a nearby stream. Working together, the women harvested a bumper crop that enabled them to support themselves and their children. Their profits also allowed them to return to SSE the original $1,200, which was then "funded forward" to provide seed money for another group of widows. Beyond this, the women had enough profits to start a tailoring business, and they have opened a retail store to sell their garments. Their first project was to create matching dresses for themselves so the world would see them as a team. Through SSE's seed money of $100 per widow, twelve families have become self-sufficient, developed a can-do team spirit, and have continued the chain of sustainable giving that is changing their community.

Sustainability changes lives. We're familiar with the saying, "Give a man a fish, and you feed him for a day; teach a man to fish, and you feed him for a lifetime." Biznistry's self-sustaining model takes this proverb one step further—it gives a person the capability of buying the fish pond. Sustainability changes the way people view themselves and the world around them, taking them from inability to capability, and from obstacles to opportunity. The promise of a steady flow of resources gives people hope, because they can move beyond thinking of just today, and start planning a future. They become part of the solution, rather than part of the problem.

Commissioned for a Kingdom Purpose

A Biznistry is a self-sustaining enterprise *commissioned for a Kingdom purpose.* To paraphrase Psalm 127, unless the Lord builds the Biznistry, its builders labor in vain. The Chairman of the Board is God himself, and those working in a Biznistry continually submit themselves to his direction and authority. God provides the inspiration, the direction, and the daily strength to accomplish the work he has planned.

Kevin Gilles, founder and CEO of 25th Hour Associates, has had to learn to surrender his strengths to God's leading. In his former position in manufacturing, he discovered he had a gift for looking futuristically, making plans three to five years ahead to grow his business. When he started his home service Biznistry, his focus began to change. "For me, the difficulty was I saw a smorgasbord of opportunities, and I wanted to eat them all. But God wasn't saying to do that," Kevin explains. "He was saying, 'Here's your portion. Focus on these I've given you.' So the biggest discovery in my faith journey is that it's not about Kevin, it's about Jesus. If He's at the center, then everything else will flourish."

Kevin also points out that a business purposed to serve God acts as a witness to customers when it provides exceptional service. "I love the Biznistry plan of releasing profits for ministry, but we have to change the way business is done as Christians," Kevin explains. "We are the light on the hill, and that light is Jesus. If people are seeing Jesus in us as we are doing our work, then they'll be more receptive to the things we're saying. If we don't have a level of excellence in the work we perform for our clients, then they don't really care what we have to say. So we want to honor our clients by giving them excellence in our work that makes them say, 'Wow! I wasn't expecting that!'"

In addition to needing God's perspective, Biznistries must also have God's passion. A Biznistry recognizes that we are in a battle for the lives of millions of hurting people and a war for the spiritual future of the world. There is no room for fear, no place for intimidation, and failure is not an option. Thus, Biznistries strive relentlessly for maximum Kingdom-building impact. We believe that God commands us to do everything in our power to use everything at our disposal to impact the lives of those in need. God's call to care for the oppressed is not a suggestion; it's a command.

When members of a Cincinnati church saw Nigerian villagers dying because of contaminated water, they didn't just shake their heads or document the disaster. They sat down with the board of Self Sustaining Enterprises and prayerfully developed a plan to form a well-digging enterprise, asking members of their congregation to provide the start-up costs. These Christians saw overwhelming need and did not shrink back from the challenge. Like Andrew facing 5,000 hungry people (John 6), they believed that Jesus would not issue a command to provide for those in need without making it possible for them to obey it. The congregation gave sacrificially, and today, a Biznistry run by Nigerians uses profits from digging wells for corporations and the wealthy to fund wells for poor villagers. As of this writing, the Biznistry has drilled 120 wells, providing clean water for 100,000 people.

Gary Dawson, founder of ReUse Centers, found his passion closer to home. His original plan was to rehab an old building, create rental spaces for contractors, and live off the rental income. But God had something else in mind. When Life Learning Center, a ministry that provides help to those seeking jobs, moved into the building, they asked if Gary might be able to provide some work for an ex-felon who had just been released from jail. God was opening a door to ministry, and Gary took his first step through that door by hiring the man to help with the ReUse Center he was setting up in the center of the building. He learned how difficult life is for those just released from prison: they have no money, so they can't pay a deposit on an apartment; they can't make money, because no one wants to hire an ex-felon.

One day Gary drove his new worker home and witnessed the miserable living quarters that were all the man could find. He was moved to find a house they could rehab so the man and others like him could get a new start. God kept opening doors, and RESET was born, a ministry that provides housing, training, work, and spiritual renewal to men recently released from prison, setting them firmly on the path of productivity and a changed life. "If these guys don't have a changed heart, all the substance abuse programs in the world won't change them," Gary says. "They've got to have a 'Come to Jesus' moment." Providing for the ex-offenders' physical needs opened the door to meeting their deep spiritual and emotional needs.

Gary has discarded his initial goal to raise retirement income through his business; all income above expenses now goes to the ministry. His passion is to develop a self-sustaining Biznistry that will continue long after he is gone, and that's what's happening. "We're not going to have a 90% recidivism rate," Gary says. "We're going to equip guys to be standard bearers. We tell them: 'It's not about you. It's about the hundreds of guys that will come after you that we'll be able to help, that will face that same thing when they walk out the prison doors, with no hope. They've burned all their bridges, their family didn't want to have anything to do with them, they have no job, they have no prospects.'" Godly passion has transformed Gary's business into a Biznistry.

Like Gary Dawson, Chuck Proudfit did not start his Skillsource business consultancy as a Biznistry, although he was committed from the beginning to follow biblical practices. Chuck made a conscious decision to transform an already "good" business into a Biznistry reflecting all of

God's greatness. When he converted the enterprise to a Biznistry, he and his staff gathered around a cross they mounted on the wall and prayed together as they committed Skillsource and its work to the Lord. The commission symbolized the business being "born again" with Christ at its center.

Operates Biblically

A Biznistry is a self-sustaining enterprise that establishes purpose from a Christian perspective, *operating according to biblical principles*. In Biznistry, the end never justifies the means. Part of the mission of a Biznistry is to provide an example of God's Kingdom in action. For example, we work hard to let our "yes be a yes"; to avoid debt that "enslaves" us to a lender; and to honor the worth of a worker's labor. Just as in life, Christians in business are called to consider others better than themselves (Phil. 2:3). This means we don't seek to crush our competition down the street; instead, we work consistent with the biblical mindset that God provides an abundance of resources, enough for us all to be successful. We act in faith, not fear, because we know that where God guides he also provides.

At the very heart of Biznistry is the conviction that we are stewards, not owners, of our resources. We entered this world with nothing, and we will leave it with nothing; what passes through our hands in between comes from God and belongs to God. He has given us time, talents, and treasures so we can serve as his hands and feet here on earth, and he will ask us for an accounting of how we have used them when we meet him in heaven. When we live out this truth, we see "our" business as God's business, and we operate under God's principles. An attitude of stewardship is the foundation of operating biblically.

Will Housh was so committed to the principle of stewardship that he named the holding company for the several family businesses he managed "Ten Talents," referring to the biblical parable. "My dad always taught me that we are managers of the resources God puts in our hand," says Will. "The name of the company is a reminder of what's most important, and a conversation starter that allows me to relate the parable in Matthew."

Because a Biznistry belongs to God, its workers must submit themselves to his leadership. According to Kevin Gilles, "Biznistry can't be simply about releasing profits. It's got to be about bringing glory and honor to Jesus in all we do, and seeking him for direction." He points out that God does not often reveal his full plan from the start. Although starting a Biznistry requires careful planning, it also requires ongoing guidance from God. "Some people want to see the whole picture," says Kevin. "But they might not get the whole picture. They might get the next step, or the next person they need to talk to. It's more about being obedient."

PASSION

Developing a "Kingdom Culture" where Christians in the marketplace function as the body of Christ, where Honor is the core value that drives purpose, function and tasks.

PURPOSE

Free clients from tasks to dedicate themselves to what's most important, while nurturing a Kingdom Culture within the organization that releases the staff to prosper within their area of gifting.

PLAN

Plan, provide and schedule services for routine home maintenance including handyman work, remodeling, painting, window & gutter cleaning, landscaping, and others, to help streamline clients' lives and give them more time for what's most important. Serve as a home and grounds service maintenance group that automatically takes care of all the routine maintenance on a client's property.

PRACTICE

Staff: Two full-time staff manage a group of contracted, dedicated service technicians, ensuring each service is completed with excellence in each of the service categories the Biznistry provides.

> "When people look at 25th Hour, it's my hope they don't see 25th Hour, they just see Jesus."
> Kevin Gilles, founder and CEO

Finances: Startup funding came from founder's personal resources. Turned a profit in the third year.

Keys to Success:

- Prompt, reliable service and response
- Prayer and obedience to the Lord
- Making relationships top priority
- Seeking the highest level of excellence in service and methods

When God is the CEO, business leadership is based on commitment and obedience to him rather than on limited human understanding. Relying on God's leading can be very freeing. At One Bistro community café, founder Robert Adamson and one other chef are the only employees—they count on volunteers for serving, greeting, bussing tables, and other tasks. Every Wednesday night One Bistro serves a free meal to over 100 people in the community. At first, Robert worried that he wouldn't have the help he needed to serve so many.

"But just before each serving session, I saw God's touch," Robert says. "People would arrive saying, 'We're here to help.' I had to step back from my management mentality. I told God, 'You're the manager. Your hands are all over this. Now I get it. I'm going to give it over to you.'" The stress that Robert used to feel in his old career as a chef drained away, and now he experiences the freedom of placing the business in God's hands and simply being an obedient servant.

Dick Gygi of ThriftSmart agrees, saying that although he is as driven as ever in his business practices, there is freedom in knowing the results are up to God. Submission and obedience to God, along with hard work, ensure that a Biznistry will be a shining example of biblical principles acting in the marketplace.

When a Biznistry faces the inevitable challenges, biblical principles provide guidance for making tough decisions. At

Skillsource, for example, an employee recently left the firm to seek a different kind of job. He resigned, but after struggling to find a new position quickly, he applied for unemployment claiming Skillsource had "discharged" him. This was not true, although his performance had caused some complications with clients. "We were faced with the dilemma of loyalty versus honesty," Chuck Proudfit explains. "We all liked this employee, wanted him to find new work, and realized that even if unemployment were granted, it would have a minimal impact financially on Skillsource. However, unemployment compensation is limited to those who have been laid off or fired, and it would have been 'bearing false witness' to remain silent on this. So, sadly, we responded to the government's inquiry, and they chose not to grant unemployment to our former employee."

A Biznistry understands that God always honors decisions based on his principles rather than on our limited human understanding.

Integrates Ministry

Biznistry is a self-sustaining enterprise that establishes purpose from a Christian perspective, operating according to biblical principles, *integrating ministry at every level*. Sound business practices guide the pursuit of Biznistry, but ministry is its ultimate goal. Employees, clients, competitors, suppliers, volunteers, and recipients of resources in the surrounding community or on the other side of the world can all be touched with the love and Christ and encouraged to achieve spiritual maturity. This doesn't mean simply requiring employees to attend Bible studies or dropping tracts in the bags of shoppers. It's more about a Biznistry functioning as the body of Christ, acting as his servants to those within its sphere of influence as it actively seeks ministry opportunities.

Biznistries live out their faith by example. "Our Christian beliefs are rooted in everything we do, every day," explains Melinda Rea, Director of Marketing at Skillsource. "The way we treat each other, serve our clients, work with our suppliers. We have come together to exemplify being a marketplace ministry, to live it. After we work for clients for a time, they simply come to know this about us, because we have a heart for service, for our clients."

In Biznistry, employees and customers come out ahead, as well as the disadvantaged people receiving support. Employees involved with Biznistry are hungry for more than business as usual. They respect and uphold the best of the business world, grounded in biblical principles. Yet they crave the extra measure of ministry that a Biznistry provides. They typically describe Biznistry as one of the most challenging *and* fulfilling of career paths, and consider it best experienced in the company of colleagues. "We want to create a freedom where people can live out their faith at work," explains Kevin Gilles of 25th Hour Associates, who encourages his employees in service and evangelism. "We want to promote Jesus."

While supervising a window & gutter cleaning crew, Kevin noticed one of the employees working on the roof was wearing a knee brace. Concerned for the man's safety, Kevin asked him what had happened. He replied that while doing roof work earlier in the week he had heard something pop in his knee, and now was unable to straighten it or bend it very far. Kevin asked him if he minded if some of the others prayed for him, and he said no, not at all. A few of them laid hands on his knee and asked the Lord to heal him. Moments later, he felt his knee getting warm. He removed the brace and said, "This feels really good," and then worked the rest of the day without the brace. "He just had an encounter with God," says Kevin. "I don't need to beat the Bible over his head; it's between him and God now. I was obedient in my part of it."

The unique ministry focus of Biznistry not only welcomes expressions of faith, it also facilitates the inclusion of non-traditional employees. The relationship of ReUse Centers with Reset ministries allows the Biznistry to serve as a training ground for recently released prisoners with felony records. One of these, who served a ten-year sentence for robbery, has been with Reset and the ReUse Center for two years and now handles the Biznistry's money. "He has access to the safe every day," says Gary Dawson. "I trust him with my life." ReUse Centers change lives by providing opportunities for those who may otherwise have none.

It's not only employees who benefit from Biznistry's focus on Christ. Customers who experience Biznistry touch a deeper spiritual reality, whether they're Christians or not. They can be assured that their experience will be one of integrity and feature quality products and services. They can look forward to thoughtful treatment by the staff, who will view them as God's children, even when they don't know it themselves. And they can rejoice in the warm feeling that comes from knowing their purchases will help benefit something or someone else, somewhere in the world, "needing the most and having the least."

Clients and customers naturally respond to the positive atmosphere of a Biznistry. The staff of New2You quickly discovered that a few customers became regulars, frequently stopping at the store to talk as much as to shop. They felt comfortable with staff members who have a heart for ministry and good people skills, and began to talk about their divorce, wayward children, or a spouse with cancer. Cheryl *(not her real name)* would often visit the thrift shop just to relax after visiting her mother at a nursing home. She had been dropping by for over a year when her mother finally died. Cheryl was experiencing the love of Christ in a business environment. Other customers have been led to Christ or begun attending church because of the influence of the Biznistry staff. Customers are invited to write down prayer requests in a notebook kept at the checkout counter, and volunteers and staff pray specifically for these needs.

The Christ-like example set by Biznistries and the top-quality goods and services they provide are, in themselves, a ministry to the local community, but Biznistries typically provide many other benefits as well. Our New2You stores serve needy local residents by accepting vouchers provided by Grace Chapel for free goods. Other Biznistries offer in-kind services, such as 25th Hour's provision of free home maintenance jobs for needy residents. The Roc-a-Fellas employees serve a free pizza lunch once a month at a local ministry for homeless men. The founders of ThriftSmart, who believe that creating jobs is the best way to help disadvantaged people, made this their first core value. The second-hand store purposely hires unskilled workers for jobs like processing donations and serving customers, providing the training they need to be effective. To further serve people in the community, ThriftSmart offers free ESL and budgeting classes, held each week right in the store.

The ministry in our international Biznistries often takes the form of meeting physical needs. SSE's chicken farming enterprise in Nigeria, for example, provides a living wage to farmers who had no regular source of income to support their families before joining the co-op. A shoemaker in Nigeria's Plateau State, a one-man Biznistry, uses his profits to make and distribute free shoes to others who cannot afford them.

Self Sustaining Enterprises

International Biznistries

H₂O Nigeria

Vineyard Community Church and SSE partnered to buy equipment for drilling deep-bore wells; the business is operated by Nigerian nationals. For every three wells drilled for paying customers, one well is provided to a village at no cost. The wells provide clean water for villages in Nigeria, greatly reducing disease and freeing children from carrying water long distances so they can attend school.

The Perfect Day Bride and Salon/Jos, Nigeria

The shop, run by two local women, rents American bridal gowns and sells costume jewelry, shoes, bridesmaid and evening dresses, and salon products to women in Jos and beyond. In partnership with a Widow's Sewing School ministry, The Perfect Day also offers traditional Nigerian wedding finery. The enterprise, as all SSE Biznistries, serves multiple purposes: jobs, ministry opportunities, and an on-going source of funds to support SSE's community development work in the village of Kisayhip and surrounding areas in Plateau State, Nigeria.

Chicken Farming/Jos, Nigeria

After raising and selling the first 200 chickens, SSE trained farmers in the area, providing much-needed jobs that pay a living wage. The farmers have formed a co-op, staggering production so they can provide a regular supply of chickens to area restaurants.

Aquaponics/Jos, Nigeria

Currently in the research and development phase, the prototype system raises fish and vegetables year-round in recirculating water. If successful, the enterprise will provide much needed protein and fresh produce for villagers, even in the dry season, as well as create jobs.

When God leads, a Biznistry may have the opportunity to proclaim Christ more directly. Recently at Skillsource, a Jewish client wanted to learn more about social enterprise. As Chuck gave her a guided tour of our local Biznistries, the client asked spiritual questions. Chuck used the God-given opportunity to answer her questions and share his personal testimony.

Our experience with ministry in a business environment is just beginning. Certainly Biznistries will find that ministry can take as many forms as there are people to serve. Through Biznistry, work becomes ministry, and business impacts lives for eternity.

Releases Funds

A Biznistry is a self-sustaining enterprise commissioned for a Kingdom purpose, operating according to biblical principles, integrating ministry at every level, and *releasing a flow of funds for further ministry advances.*

A Biznistry recognizes that God ultimately owns everything, and he makes it a privilege to be stewards of the resources he entrusts to us. Thus, Biznistries reinvest profits for the common good, rather than hoard profits for a select few. The parable of the talents in Matthew 25:14-30 helps us to realize that all that we have is given to us by God and all of it should be used to glorify him. This perspective profoundly affects our attitude toward the choices we make, how we conduct business, and how we give.

Biznistry leaders understand they are stewards of resources that belong to God, so they want to be sure they are used in an effective and godly manner. As Dick Gygi developed ThriftSmart, he and his partners determined to avoid the pitfalls of traditional funding for ministries. "Non-profits generally are run by people who have passion for their cause, but no training or experience leading an organization," Dick explains. "They jump in and do it without a model or operating framework, resulting in a lot of trial and error, and extending the learning curve." To avoid this wastefulness, Dick and his partners traveled coast-to-coast studying thrift stores all over the country to see what worked and what didn't. They recorded all the best practices they discovered, and from this research created an operating model for their stores. This model not only shortened the learning curve for staff in the first stores they opened, but also provided a handbook to equip franchises throughout the country with practical guidelines for success.

Biznistries choose operating strategies that will provide the maximum amount of profit for contribution to their targeted causes. Our New2You thrift store in Mason, Ohio is housed in a building that used to be a drab warehouse. We chose to renovate it with bright lights, paint, inexpensive but sturdy racks and furnishings from a large retail store that was closing, and lots of volunteer labor. While making the interior bright, spacious, and inviting, we purposely kept the warehouse look with its exposed fixtures not only for its hip urban style, but also to stretch our resources so we could maximize profit for giving. Changes and additions to the store are made only when we determine that they will both increase business and increase profits for ministry.

A *flow of funds* for ministry is what sets a Biznistry apart from a business that periodically gives to charity. Rather than viewing contribution as something nice we can do when the funds are available, Biznistries make their business decisions with prayerful thought to providing a consistent, ongoing source of funds to its ministries. This source of reliable funding allows a ministry to create a plan to work toward its vision, rather than subsisting day to day.

A Biznistry may channel profits to one designated ministry, such as ReUse Centers providing funding for Reset Ministries, a recovery program for ex-convicts, or to several ministries. Over the years Chuck Proudfit has donated hundreds of thousands of dollars from Skillsource profits for ministry work ranging from micro-enterprises to job retraining to At Work On Purpose, the work life ministry he founded. The strategic focus of all his giving is marketplace ministry, because it is both Chuck's passion and an area of ministry that is typically neglected. Hundreds of micro-enterprises in the under-resourced nations of Nigeria, India, and Mexico have been created with funding from Skillsource, lifting thousands of people out of poverty with a "hand up" rather than a "handout," representing another form of marketplace ministry.

Biznistries operate with open hands, accepting all the resources God provides, stewarding them responsibly, and then releasing the profits to make a difference in the lives of others.

Is Biznistry Social Enterprise?

One of the biggest changes in the marketplace in the last twenty years is the rise of social enterprise. According to the Social Enterprise Alliance (SEA), social enterprise is "an organization or venture within an organization that advances a social mission through market-based strategies. These strategies include receiving earned income in direct exchange for a product, service, or privilege."[1] Many Christians today are attracted to social enterprise because of its positive, selfless goals, the sense of purpose it promotes, and the opportunity it offers to make a difference in the lives of others. Social Enterprise, for our purposes, is at the peak of the Better Business category.

The recent explosion of social enterprise is a global phenomenon, and for good reason. The growth of this marketplace sector, says the SEA, is a response to "shrinking government budgets, employment rolls, and social safety nets." Traditional institutions, as we have seen, are no longer enough to meet the needs of the world, and social enterprise addresses these concerns

- **more efficiently than government**, which no longer has the mandate or resources to solve every social problem;
- **more sustainably and creatively than the nonprofit sector**, which faces declining funding streams and increased demands for innovation, proof of what works and collaboration; and
- **more generously than business**, which is mandated to place pre-eminence on shareholder returns.[2]

Biznistry shares these claims, for Biznistry functions in many ways as a social enterprise. The difference, of course, comes when we focus on a key phrase in our Biznistry definition: *commissioned for a Kingdom purpose.*

Biznistry can be called a *Christian* social enterprise, but the difference goes far beyond tacking a qualifier on to a general concept. From a biblical perspective, social enterprise is not selling out, but it *is* selling short. It is the *purpose* of Biznistry that sets it apart from social enterprise, and purpose is the very foundation of any organization.

The Social Enterprise Alliance says, "Our goal is nothing less than to change the world for the common good." Common good is a worthy goal, and certainly Christians should be concerned for the good of those beyond themselves. But sometimes *good* can be the enemy of *great*, and Christians have been given a Great Commission, not a Good Commission. Our purpose is also to change the world—not just for the common good, but to advance the Kingdom of God. This foundational difference of purpose is at the very heart of Biznistry.

Biznistries, from the beginning, are built under God's direction for the express purpose of glorifying and serving him, and evangelism, discipleship, and worship are integral aspects of every Biznistry. Those Christians who start and develop Biznistries are conscious that "unless the Lord builds the house, its builders labor in vain."[3] Good work is *just* that—good. If it loses its connection with God and does not proclaim Christ, it does not fulfill the Great Commission. Certainly individual Christians can glorify God as they work within a social enterprise, or in any Better Business, just as they can in Biznistry. But in Biznistry, the very *organization* is intentionally built to glorify God, and this fundamental difference creates new and greater opportunities to advance his Kingdom.

Notes

[1]"What's a Social Enterprise?" Social Enterprise Alliance, 2012.
<https://www.se-alliance.org/why#whatsasocialenterprise>

[2]*Ibid.*

[3]Psalms 127:1

4

Building a Biznistry

God's work done God's way will never lack God's supply. – J.
Hudson Taylor

Jerry couldn't wait to share his vision for a thrift store to
finance well-digging in Africa with his wife. As he helped
Sarah rinse the dinner dishes and load the dishwasher, he
told her about the woman gleaning from the trash at the curb
that morning as he left for work. Soon they were sitting at
the table again, and Jerry was speaking with an intensity
Sarah had not heard for a long time. This was something big,
and Sarah gave Jerry her full attention.

"Can't you see it?" Jerry asked excitedly. "Customers will
know they're in a different kind of business as soon as they
walk in. People will want to donate their unwanted items
when they know the profits will be helping needy people.
We'll hire Christians, and the staff can pray together each day
before we open."

"Isn't that discrimination? Is that legal?" Sarah asked.

"I think so, if it's a small business. I guess I'd need some legal advice."

"What about a building?"

"I've been thinking about that. There's that empty place on Park Street where the craft store went under. It needs a lot of work, but I think we can recruit some volunteers."

"But you've still got to pay for it," Sarah said gently. "Where's the money going to come from?"

Jerry sighed. Of course, he had thought about this already. "Maybe we could interest a Christian entrepreneur who could provide the capital," he said hopefully. "Of course, he'd have to realize that he's not going to see a personal return, since profits will go to the well-digging operation."

Jerry paused. Somehow the possibility seemed more remote than when he had first thought of it.

"Maybe a bank loan would work better," suggested Sarah.

"But then we'd be committing our profits first to pay it back," said Jerry. "That would take years. What about the wells?"

"Talk to Pastor Ken," advised Sarah. "He might have some ideas, and certainly he could get the church behind the project."

"I don't know how the church will respond," said Jerry. "I'm sure some people won't think the church ought to be getting involved in business, even one with a Christian foundation."

"It would be a great way to provide a job for Keisha," said Sarah. Keisha was the single mom in their church who was looking for work. "Certainly the congregation would be excited to be able to provide her with a job."

"Well, I would hope so, but people are funny, Sarah. They get set in their ways and aren't always receptive to new ways of doing things."

Jerry's excitement was fading as he and Sarah discussed the practical aspects of the enterprise he envisioned. A building, capital, legal issues, employees, competition, church support... the list was daunting. Yet the spark still burned deep inside Jerry, a spark he felt sure was from God.

Let's be real: starting a Biznistry is neither fast nor easy. A new venture may take a year or more to become profitable, depending on the nature of the business, and only about half of new employer establishments survive at least five years.[1] As the Biznistry movement gathers momentum, and statistics emerge, we would anticipate results similar to those of the general marketplace. In other words, it takes *time and discipline* for a Biznistry to become profitable. Unlike charities, which solicit donations and can immediately apply them to the target need, Biznistry leaders face a start-up phase that may last months or even years before they see profits applied to a cause. They sacrifice an immediate return for the greater goals of sustainability and growth. Those involved in Biznistry must have faith that overcomes the fear of starting out when profits are a distant hope. This is another reason why those considering Biznistry must be sure they are following God's lead, and be committed for the long haul.

Biznistry leaders must have both "a tough mind and a tender heart," qualities described in Martin Luther King, Jr.'s sermon of the same name. Blending and balancing these seeming opposites may be the most difficult challenge facing a Biznistry, but it's a challenge that Jesus himself presented to his disciples when he sent them out into a hostile world. "I am sending you out like sheep among wolves," Jesus said. "Therefore be as shrewd as snakes and as innocent as doves."[2] Biznistry leaders must have both the tender heart that discerns the needs of people and responds in compassion, and the tough mind that relentlessly seeks the best and most efficient methods of running a disciplined business.

Nehemiah's Approach

It wasn't a business Nehemiah was seeking to run over 2,500 years ago, but he faced many of the same challenges as he sought to rebuild the broken walls of Jerusalem. His tough mind and tender heart guided him as he led a successful but challenging enterprise, and the godly characteristics of his leadership—prayer, passion, planning, persistence, and purity—set a timeless example for those building Biznistries today.

Passion

King David's great city, where Solomon had built the Temple to the Lord's specific instructions, was desolate. God's people had been exiled to foreign lands, and many had not survived. Now a remnant of the exiles was returning to Jerusalem, and Nehemiah, cupbearer to the king of Persia, was anxious to know how they and the city fared. "Those who survived the exile and are back in the province are in great trouble and disgrace," his brother Hanani told him when he returned from a visit there. "The wall of Jerusalem is broken down, and its gates have been burned with fire."[3]

Nehemiah's heart broke. He immediately sat down and wept, and from that moment his life changed. For "some days" he mourned and fasted and prayed;[4] there was nothing more important to him than the renewal of God's people and their holy city. Nehemiah's passion and despair were evident even to the king, who said to him, "Why does your face look so sad when you are not ill? This can be nothing but sadness of heart."[5]

Passion can fall on us like fire, as it did for Nehemiah, or it can begin as a tiny spark that over time grows into a hot blaze. Godly enterprises begin with godly passion, and passion begins deep in the heart.

Prayer

It didn't take long before Nehemiah's despondency birthed his desire for action. And because every godly enterprise must begin with prayer, Nehemiah's first consultant was God. He began by confessing the sins of himself and his people, and then reminded God of his promise to gather the exiles and return them to the land if they would repent and obey his commands. In this way, Nehemiah assured that he was approaching God on his own terms and submitting to his plan. Only then did he ask God for success in his first action step of approaching the king.[6]

Nehemiah continued to pray throughout the enterprise—before he explained his desire to his employer, the king; during the building, especially when he faced opposition; and when the walls were complete, to praise God for his provision. God's work must be done God's way, and constant communication with him is the foundation on which any godly enterprise is based.

Planning

Nehemiah's careful planning for his enterprise began with obtaining permission from his current employer for leave from his position to direct the rebuilding of Jerusalem's walls. Once he had the king's approval, he determined the amount of time his enterprise would take. Then he asked for letters for safe passage through foreign lands, and to obtain timber for building.[7] Once in Jerusalem, Nehemiah carefully examined the walls and the gates to determine the work that would be needed. He enlisted the necessary workers and gave them each an appointed task.[8] Failure to plan any one of these tasks might have meant failure for the whole enterprise. In the same way, development of a careful, well-thought-out business plan is essential to the success of a startup Biznistry. Yes, the work is done with God's guidance and strength—Nehemiah told the workers "about the gracious hand of God" upon him[9]—but providence and planning must go hand-in-hand for success.

Persistence

Even the best advance planning can't anticipate every obstacle a new enterprise will face. Nehemiah and the Israelites "rebuilt the wall till all of it reached half its height, for the people worked with all their heart." But then the neighboring rulers heard that Jerusalem was once more becoming a protected, inhabited city, and they didn't like it; in fact, "they all plotted together to come and fight against Jerusalem and stir up trouble against it," and the Jews who lived near them told those in Jerusalem they would surely be attacked. About the same time, the returning exiles said, "The strength of the laborers is giving out, and there is so much rubble that we cannot rebuild the wall."[10]

Opposition, fatigue, and discouragement are a killer trio—and any new enterprise can expect to face these sooner or later. Nehemiah met these obstacles with persistence tempered with prayer. First, he posted armed guards to protect the workers and the half-built walls. Then, he encouraged his workers: "Don't be afraid of them. Remember the Lord, who is great and awesome, and fight for your brothers, your sons and your daughters, your wives and your homes." They returned to the work, but some changes had to be made. Nehemiah put half the men to work on the wall; the other half he armed heavily to protect the workers.[11]

Like Nehemiah, successful Biznistry leaders make careful changes in the original business plan when needed to ensure success. Most of all, a Biznistry must overcome opposition, fatigue, discouragement, and unexpected change with godly passion and persistence to accomplish its God-given purpose.

Purity

Times were tough in Nehemiah's day. Food was scarce and the king's tax was high; some families even had to sell their children as slaves in order to survive. Especially demeaning was the high interest wealthier Jews were charging the needy on loans. Nehemiah confronted the nobles and officials with righteous indignation: "You are exacting usury from your own countrymen!...What you are doing is not right. Shouldn't you walk in the fear of our God to avoid the reproach of our Gentile enemies?"[12]

He brought the unbiblical practices of the wealthy to an abrupt halt, and demanded they give restitution to the poor. As governor, he also set a higher standard for himself, not taking the taxes and food previous governors had demanded from the people while he devoted himself to the work God had given him.[13] Nehemiah understood that God's work must be done God's way to be successful and pleasing to him. Biznistries, too, operate under the highest possible standards—God's own. Refusing to compromise the purity of biblical principles honors God and demonstrates his character in the Biznistry's sphere of influence.

Nehemiah's tender heart launched his passion, turned him to God, and guided his leadership. His tough mind assessed all aspects of the work, carefully planned a course of action, anticipated difficulties, and persevered to overcome problems. These same qualities are what make a Biznistry successful today.

For new Biznistry ventures, being tough-minded in business begins by exploring a product or service concept, and then continues by determining its viability in a competitive marketplace. Just as any business, a Biznistry must have a better product and a better plan to succeed, even when success is measured in ministry as well as money. Many concepts are not strong enough to endure close inspection, but the strongest attract seed capital for a launch.

PASSION

Modeling biblical values and godly stewardship while providing for "the least of these."

PURPOSE

Develop a culture of stewardship and giving in a business community; provide financial support for ministries such as Back2Back that help orphans and impoverished children break free from the cycle of generational poverty.

PLAN

Provide exceptional customer service through a family of websites offering a wide range of trade-related products like filters, humidifiers, spot coolers, dehumidifiers, thermostats, furnace and air conditioner repair parts, registers, exhaust fans, and much more.

PRACTICE

Staff: A staff of 12 serves in management, customer service, order fulfillment, marketing, business development, and accounting.

> "God has the method all figured out; it's up to us to apply it."
>
> Founder and CEO Will Housh

Finances: Owner Will Housh applied his knowledge and experience from the family heating and air conditioning business as he started the first of several e-commerce sites in 2006. His success in this venture allowed him to sell the other businesses to family members and concentrate on Housh, Inc. He avoids debt, and contributes a minimum of 10% of profits to ministry.

Keys to Success:

- Seeks to provide a "customer wow" experience by exceeding expectations
- Treats customers with integrity, practicing the Golden Rule
- Superior knowledge and experience developed over three generations
- Guarantees lowest Web pricing, fast shipping, and great customer service

Once underway, the best of the new ventures stay true to the overall growth plan and foundational principles, but also adopt practices readily based on marketplace response. The early years are often the hardest, a proverbial "fire" in which fledgling Biznistries are shaped and reshaped for sustainable success in both profits and ministry.

The Raw Materials

The Inspiration

Before the work comes the vision, and before the vision, the inspiration. Because Biznistry at its best is God's work done God's way, its inspiration must ultimately be from God. Starting a Biznistry takes commitment and dedication—first to God, and then to the vision he gives. Biznistry is a *calling*, not a "holy hobby." You can't just dabble with your toes to test the water; you've got to be confident physically, emotionally, and spiritually that God is calling you to dive in.

Biznistry requires passion. Over and over, those involved in Biznistry tell us it's passion for the defined purpose of the Biznistry that drives their success. One of the passions that drove us to establish many of our Biznistries began when Jeff encountered orphans in Mexico and the poor in Nigeria (described in the Introduction). "God commands us in the Psalms, 'Defend the cause of the weak and fatherless;

maintain the rights of the poor and oppressed. Rescue the weak and needy; deliver them from the hand of the wicked,'" says Jeff. "I don't believe that God would command us to serve the needy without giving us the means to do it. For us, Biznistry became the means to help those we were passionate about."

Your passion may be very different than Jeff's. Dick Gygi and the founders of ThriftSmart wanted to erase economic, cultural and racial barriers in education, so one of the beneficiaries of ThriftSmart's profits is New Hope Academy, a racially and economically diverse Christian school in Tennessee. Gary Dawson became passionate about providing opportunities for men recently released from prison after getting to know one of them who began to work for him. Gary wasn't looking to start a ministry at the time, but the passion sparked by his experience now provides the fuel to fulfill the vision God has given him. Brad Rogers, who grew up on a farm in Indiana, is passionate about growing healthy food and sharing it with others. His passion is leading him to develop a space-saving aquaponics facility in urban Cincinnati that will reconnect people in "food deserts" with locally-grown, nutritious food.

If you haven't yet discovered your passion, consider SSE director Pete West's question: "What thing do you do that *creates* energy rather than *drains* energy?" Your answer will give you insight into the passion God has given you.

Whatever part of God's work he is calling you to do, that will be the foundation of your Biznistry. The marketable business idea will be the engine to fuel that cause.

The People

Jerry had years of experience promoting sales while making wise spending decisions. He had some specific ideas for how to make a thrift store popular and profitable in his community. But he sensed these were not enough—he'd have to be the right person to make the enterprise successful. He had the passion, but he knew that startup businesses faced daunting challenges, and many did not succeed. How did he know if God was really calling him to turn his vision into reality? And if he was the right one to lead this effort, he knew he needed to surround himself with a network of supportive people who shared his passion, provided guidance in areas outside his expertise, and contributed wisdom and resources not only for the startup but also throughout the growth of the enterprise. Before the right building and funding, Jerry's Biznistry would need the right people.

God has endowed his people with a vast variety of gifts to be used in service to him and to others. When traditional businesses are hiring, they focus rather narrowly on a particular type of person or skill set for a given job. Biznistries, on the other hand, can embrace a much wider range of people and skills because of their unique view of business and ministry. We are open to non-traditional workers and ideas if they move us toward God's goals for our enterprise.

When Jim Mullaney shared his vision for a Biznistry that would fund outreach ministries of his church with his pastor and a few other church members, the type of business was not as important to him as its purpose. Together his team brainstormed a list of 31 possible enterprises before settling on a kettle corn booth that would travel to a variety of local weekend festivals and fairs. It was not until the team got down to details that they fully realized how God had guided the selection of both the enterprise and the leadership team, which became Amaizing Grace Kettle Corn's board of directors.

"Every one of us brought something to the table, and it wouldn't have worked if this particular talent or resource wasn't there," says Jim. One of the board members is a musician who performs at festivals, so he is helpful in identifying and contacting festivals appropriate for the kettle corn booth. Another has mechanical ability, and cares for the equipment and built a trailer for transporting it. Jim, founder and president of a business service company for 14 years, provided expertise in entrepreneurship and creating a business plan. His company has a phone team that the Biznistry uses to help find festivals.

One board member has a business degree and a passion for business, as well as a pickup truck that was essential for hauling the equipment before the Biznistry had a trailer. Also the finance head of the church, this board member gave validity to the enterprise in the eyes of the congregation. Pastor Valerie Waibel's position provided support when the Biznistry met opposition, as she spoke up for the importance of taking a risk and following Jesus' lead by going into the marketplace to make disciples. She also leads in bringing the ministry aspects of the Biznistry into focus, balancing Jim's business perspective. The board's final member, along with his other abilities, brought something unexpected. When the board realized they would need a place to store their trailer and equipment, he said, "No problem; I have a small airplane hangar." God had thought of every detail.

Clearly, people are the heart of an organization; in fact, the organization *is* the people. It is often less challenging to fund a Biznistry than it is to find the special people who make a Biznistry thrive. Every Biznistry needs to start with a leader, someone who understands the depths of what it means to be in Biznistry. This is a person with both a head for business, and a heart for ministry. This is a person who is truly called to a leadership role, not someone who is entering Biznistry simply as a new career step. This is a person who can navigate the nuances of delivering best business practices and best ministry practices *at the same time,* even when they sometimes seem to conflict. Effective Biznistry leaders are sensitive and compassionate, but tough-minded in their business skills.

green
recycling
wCrks

PASSION
Recovering addicts graduating from City Gospel Mission's year-long residential program need guidance and practice in developing job skills so they can transition to a productive life.

PURPOSE
"To reclaim lives as we reclaim materials."

PLAN
Service the recycling needs of local businesses by providing, for a modest fee, collection containers and pickup service for paper, cardboard, plastics, clothing, aluminum, books, and carpet; sell gathered materials to recycling companies. The enterprise provides both job experience and funds for the non-profit's recovery program.

PRACTICE
Staff: Director; up to ten graduates of CGM's drug rehab program, each employed for one year.

Finances: Start-up costs provided by business and individual donations; business plan calls for self-sustainability in three years or business will close.

> "Our goal is to get guys transferred back into regular employment. It's more than just providing a job; we're deeply involved in their lives."
>
> Director Matthew Long

Keys to Success:
- Nature of the work requires simple skills, allowing men of any background to participate with minimal training, and appropriate for the planned transiency of the enterprise.
- Recycling provides two streams of income: businesses pay for the service, recycling companies pay for the materials
- Director's experience in business, education, and pastoring allow him to guide employees in business skills, life skills, and practical issues such as obtaining driver's licenses and resolving past legal matters.

Because a Biznistry is doing God's work, those who guide it must be committed to him and understand the spiritual principles on which it is based, as well as have a faith that will allow them to submit to God's guidance even when it seems to counter rational understanding. In our Biznistries, we have required the senior leadership to be growing Christians. They have God's heart through the Holy Spirit, and consistently demonstrate spiritual maturity blended with business skills from their employment history. Generally, those called by God to lead in Biznistry demonstrate both in word and action a humble heart of service and sacrifice. We do employ non-Christians for some staff roles, viewing this as an opportunity to be living witnesses for Christ through the impact of our working environment.

In short, successful Biznistry leaders are a rare breed. They are capable (have necessary skills); available (willing to redirect careers into callings); and compatible (willing to accept the ministry dimensions of the task, which may mean earning less income, occasionally hiring "second chance" people, spending extra time with customers, or other "sacrifices").

Retirees as a resource. Although finding the right people to lead a Biznistry is challenging, we have seen that many people are attracted to Biznistry as they seek a way to serve God with the skills and experience they've gained after working for years in traditional business. Many experienced workers see retirement as not when you stop working, but when you change ministry. Pete West, recently retired after working thirty years for a large manufacturer of consumer goods, is one of these. He explains, "We're living in a time when second careers are realistic options. In past generations, you worked until you couldn't work anymore, and that was it. Now floating off into the sunset is no longer the only retirement paradigm."

As a projects manager for Procter & Gamble, Pete was stationed twice overseas. In both Europe and South America, he got to know many missionaries who had to raise their own support. This took a large chunk of their time. Some were not good at it; some grew discouraged and frustrated about finances and left the ministry. He thought there must be a better way to fund their work than to continually seek donations.

Retirees who serve in Biznistries bring their intellectual capital—their wisdom and experience—to lend to others. Pete didn't have traditional training for "full-time" ministry when he left his corporate job, but he recognized his skills and experience as resources that could be used in God's service. He wasn't ready to settle for a sedentary lifestyle, and he had enough savings that the purpose of his work mattered more to him than financial income. In short, he wanted to work to serve the Lord, and he really didn't need more money. Now, Pete is Director of Self Sustaining Enterprises in the U.S. The back of his SSE business card sums up Pete's new position: "Combining a head for business with a heart for ministry."

He explains why he made the change: "Marketplace ministry is an unconventional strategy that can dramatically change the ways we do things, but it needs passionate people to drive it. I realized I could be one of those passionate people." Pete, through his leadership at SSE, wants to move the marketplace ministry movement farther down the road. He believes that building an ethical, biblical model for how to run an enterprise creates a counter-culture in the business world.

Pete sees himself as representing a new group of people who can work in Christian ministry without needing the financial support from others that traditional missionaries and pastors require. He explains that his years of work experience and the benefits he enjoys in retirement allow him to become essentially a self-sufficient minister. "Your salary is all paid, and your benefits are all covered, and your travel expenses are on your own," he explains. "I can work free of charge, so my employment doesn't put a financial burden on an organization." Fewer salaried workers, of course, means more funds freed up for ministry.

"It's a form of volunteerism," he says. "But it's a little different, because it's not just free labor—that's great—but it also takes the skills and talents and experience that people have from a career vocation and uses them for ministry activities." In embracing retiring business people, Self

Sustaining Enterprises has tapped into an underdeveloped resource to increase its ministry.

Knocked down to be built up. Dave and Amber Stacy's story is very different. Both come from difficult family backgrounds, and both began working while in their teens. Dave's strong work ethic meant he always had a job, and he and Amber eventually ran their own courier company. "I'd be working 12 to 14 hours, and I did night runs; she would be in the next state," Dave says. "We would take on extra routes. We were doing well financially, but we weren't spending much time together. There was money left over after paying the bills, but at what cost? You never stop to think why you're doing it. We were losing touch with what's really important, and running ourselves into the ground. What kind of a marriage is it when you only spend 15 to 20 minutes together in a day?"

Then God grabbed their attention. When Dave came down with what he thought was the flu, he stopped at the V.A. medical center to be checked out. It turned out he had double pneumonia—as well as a rare form of flu. He was admitted to the hospital and began treatment, but he only got worse. After more than a week, the doctor pulled Amber aside. "We've done everything we can," he told her. "Either the pneumonia or the flu is going to get him. Does he have a living will?"

But people at their church began to pray, and Dave started getting better. "I don't care how good the doctors are, how good the hospital is; they're not really in charge," says Dave. "They don't have the final say-so."

Less than a week after the doctor's discussion with Amber, Dave was discharged from the hospital. He became winded just walking across a room, and he had to have an oxygen tank everywhere he went. Doctors feared his heart and lungs would never fully recover.

But week by week he grew stronger, and at his two-month follow-up visit the doctors found no lung damage and said he had the heart of a bull. In a difficult economy, Dave finally found work at barely over minimum wage. Then he blew out his knee, and got cellulitis in that leg. He went on Workman's Comp and his employer had to let him go.

When he was able, Dave re-entered a tight job market and for the first time could not find work. "They're interviewing this six-foot, muscular young college graduate," says Dave, "and then here comes this short, 50-plus old guy with white hair and a limp who's gained 60 pounds from being on his butt not able to work for two years. Who are they going to hire?" A man who had always worked hard, almost never missing a day, was out of the workforce for a total of two and a half years.

Amber says, "As a wife, it's hard to see your husband struggle with the fact that he can't provide for his family, and it's not for lack of wanting to—he physically cannot do it."

"Mentally, emotionally, I was losing my mind," adds Dave.

But spiritually? That's another story entirely. Not long before Dave got sick, he and Amber had given their lives to Christ. "The difference Christ has made in my life…" Dave's eyes fill with tears. "I can't talk about it. I've never had anything in my life move me like the walk the last five years has been. The time when the best thing came into my life, my life took a turn for what other people would consider the worst. But I told my pastor, 'I will take a bad day in the light over a good day in the darkness.' My whole life prior to meeting Amber and the two of us coming to Christ together was in the dark.

"Someone once told me that when you turn on a flashlight outside on a sunny day, you can't see the light. But when you take the flashlight into a dark cave, it looks like the sun exploded. From the life I led, and who I used to be, to this inside of me now—it's powerful."

So when Pastor Jeff approached Dave and Amber with an opportunity to own and run a coffee kiosk Biznistry, they saw God's hand at work. "I never had a desire to be a barista," says Dave. "I still don't. But here was a business someone could run, and I needed a job. I've got the work ethic; I needed somewhere to channel it. I didn't have two nickels to rub together. And it's endorsed by the church I've grown to love."

Dave and Amber dove in headfirst, learning all about the coffee business and applying sweat equity to renovate and set up the kiosk that has become Sunrise Coffee. Dave even designed the logo himself.

"This is something I never dreamed about doing in a million years," Dave says. "But our view and God's view—they can be so different. I worked my whole life, I got knocked down, and finally I said, 'I surrender.' That's when, all of a sudden, boom, here comes a coffee shop."

Team spirit. No matter how the leader comes to Biznistry, he or she will need a team for sustainable success. Even for the simplest Biznistry with just one person working alone, a "community" team of Biznistry-minded colleagues is indispensable for guidance, encouragement and accountability. Guidance is important so that the leader can make tough decisions with the added wisdom of others immersed in Biznistry.[14] Encouragement is important because Satan desires to attack any enterprise dedicated to God's glory,[15] and a team can help spotlight some of the joy in the suffering.[16] Accountability is important because the world continually tempts us to compromise,[17] yet a Biznistry can settle for nothing less than the best practices in both business and ministry.

Biznistries generally start out small, so it's especially important they have the right people in the right place. A company with a hundred employees may not be much affected by one who is in the wrong job; a Biznistry of only three people cannot survive if one of them is not a good fit. Having the right people in place often makes the difference in overcoming, rather than collapsing under, a tough situation. Our enterprises would never have succeeded if not for a group of people who so believed in what they were doing that they wouldn't let it fail. A leader has to be passionate and relentless; those surrounding him or her must have the same attitude. Our Biznistries are successful not because of any individual, but because of the sacrificial, never-give-up attitude of a number of passionate people.

Finding people passionate about their work is increasingly rare, especially in a difficult economy. Heather is doing a great job entering data in a computer, but she dreads Monday mornings. Steve gets satisfactory performance reviews from his boss at the utility company, but he feels his work doesn't best use his skills. When Kevin Gilles started 25th Hour Associates, he wanted to be sure he had the right people in the right place. "We wanted people who saw the vision of the Biznistry and worked within their gifting," he explains.

Kevin finds ability tests and personality assessments helpful in placing the right people in the right job, but these omit the spiritual component. Kevin says it's important to consider both natural abilities and spiritual gifts when matching a potential employee with a job; he's trying out a new test that encompasses both. "If I'm hiring an office manager, I want to encompass all of her gifting for the benefit of the organization," Kevin explains. "If she has the gift of discernment, and she's answering the phone, she may put a client on hold and tell me, 'Kevin, I don't know what's going on, but something just isn't right.'" The office manager's discernment may uncover a business problem or an opportunity for ministry. "Within our business, we want to empower people and release them to prosper in what they do," Kevin sums up. The right people in the right position mean dedicated workers committed to a Biznistry's vision as well as a more smoothly functioning business.

When Mike Stretch felt God was calling him to begin a graphic design Biznistry, he wasn't alone. Valerie Hoffman, a coworker at his former company, had begun thinking in Biznistry terms before she even heard the concept. The projects she got most excited about were those that had a mission emphasis. "I wanted to partner with people who had a similar mission rather than making things look pretty," she explains. Valerie had the capability, the availability, *and* the compatibility with the Biznistry's purpose. They believe God brought them together, and Mike appreciates how their resources and skills complement each other. Valerie, young and only a few years out of college, did not have the business expertise or capital to move into her own business, but she wanted someday to do this. Mike had the resources and business experience, but needed help. Mike invested in Valerie, looking beyond the immediate: "If she can grow here and say she learned from the old man, that's part of what I'm doing here," he says. He understands that his role as a Biznistry leader includes helping his coworkers develop both professionally and spiritually.

Finding the right people is not easy, and keeping them may not be, either. Most startup businesses will have to face difficult adjustments in staff that deeply affect people's lives. "This has been the hardest, most painful part of our start up," says Kevin Gilles of 25th Hour Associates. "We started out with three full-time employees, grew to nine, and then through a series of events and restructuring we are down to two staff members." The best business plan cannot foresee changes in the marketplace, economic downturns, or all the "people issues" that may arise. When facing staffing difficulties, Kevin stresses the importance of an attitude of Honor. "We need to see the Glory in others, without stumbling over who they are not," he explains. "We are all in a process."

The Product

The inspiration for a Biznistry comes when we least expect it, or from years of study and contemplation. Jerry found his inspiration at a dusty African orphanage. His business idea, however, began near a trash can on his pre-dawn suburban street. A Biznistry business idea can come from anyone, anywhere, but you'll want to be sure it offers you the greatest opportunity for success. So begin by examining your passions and prayerfully seeking God's will. He helps us find our way in life as we listen to the word of God in the Bible, the Spirit of God within us, and the people of God around us. The spark for Biznistry comes in as many ways as there are people committed to serving God through their work. Whether it comes through our circumstances, our experiences, our talents, our resources, or simply through our availability, God provides the idea and direction to those he calls to Biznistry.

We have found it helpful to gather a group of creative, entrepreneurial people for "think tank" sessions, brainstorming ideas for new Biznistries and ways to expand existing Biznistries in the marketplace. The individuals in our Innovate group, many of them young entrepreneurs, share ideas that often build on each other, producing innovative strategies that might elude any single member. They also provide a source of instant feedback, encouragement, and support.

Regardless of how they first appear, the best Biznistry concepts share five key traits:

1. Simple: not too complicated, so it can be brought to market with relative ease
2. Affordable: not too expensive, so that many investors can start one
3. Profitable: a reliable money maker, so that ministry funding is consistent

4. Replicable: reproducible by others, so that the concept can be a broader blessing

5. Fruitful: providing opportunities for ministry, so customers, employees, suppliers and others may be touched with the love of Christ

Consider the thrift store industry. The basic premise is simple: take in tax-deductible donated items, and then resell them for a profit. Each New2You location requires about $60,000 of seed capital. God has blessed our efforts, and our initial store has been consistently profitable from the launch year forward. The New2You thrift store model has also been systematized, so we can replicate it anywhere in the United States.

In considering Biznistry concepts, it's important to remember that the enterprise which finally emerges should serve three groups of stakeholders with excellence:

1. Customers, from consistently high quality products and services;

2. Employees, from fulfilling employment opportunities at competitive rates of pay;

3. The disadvantaged, from a sustainable flow of funds through Biznistry profits.

These stakeholders, along with suppliers, competitors, and the community at large, become the "congregation," the ministry venue, of the Biznistry.

ReUse Centers

PASSION

Ex-offenders need housing, job experience, and a Christ-centered transitional program that offers a second chance at leading a productive life.

PURPOSE

Provide financial support for Reset Ministries, a live-in, comprehensive transitional program for ex-offenders; provide transitional, guided employment for men in the program.

PLAN

Reclaim building-grade products from company overstocks, donations, and building deconstructions and resell them at affordable prices to those rehabbing or repairing homes and buildings. Profits support Reset Ministries, and the business provides employment for men in the program.

PRACTICE

Staff: 12 full-time, 6 part time; many are ex-offenders

Finances: Old downtown warehouse building that houses the enterprise's original location was acquired with no money up front and rehabbed by the staff; rental income from more than 20 business and ministry tenants pays building expenses. Items for sale are donated or gleaned from condemned buildings, so expenses are primarily for transportation.

> "I can see the good coming from this, the lives changed. It's a God thing, because I know it has very little to do with me."
>
> Director Gary Dawson

Keys to Success:

- Partnerships with companies and the city provide resources and work opportunities
- Staff and board members represent a variety of skills
- The staff and ex-offenders form close relationships based on trust
- Business depends on God's one-step-at-a-time leading and learning from mistakes

The Plan

Every Biznistry starts with a great idea, but not every great idea can become a Biznistry. Like any business idea, it must stand up to rigorous study and planning to show it can be profitable. A football coach wouldn't start a season without a playbook and expect to win. Sure, he might add or subtract plays as the season progresses, or tweak some to make them work better, but he'll work with that initial book until it's dog-eared and ragged. In the same way, every Biznistry must begin with a comprehensive, rigorous business plan. A godly foundation, good intentions, and giving to charity don't bring in customers by themselves; a Biznistry must offer a better product at a better price, with excellent customer service, to succeed.

A thorough plan starts with considering the SWOTs of the potential business: its Strengths, Weaknesses, Opportunities, and possible Threats. Get to know your potential customers by listening and examining demographics; survey best practices in the industry by studying successful competitors. The practices initiated for a Biznistry's playbook must pass approval by a higher authority than those of a traditional business, for a Biznistry expects to be blessed by God. It must establish and act under biblical principles in obtaining and applying resources, finding a suitable venue, hiring the right people, and serving its customers.

For example, the Bible is clear that where God leads, he abundantly provides. This spiritual reality is directly counter to the "scarcity mentality" common in the traditional business world, where enterprises fight to get a large enough share of limited resources to avoid going out of business. Rather than being driven by the fear that underlies this scarcity mindset, Biznistries are driven by faith. Our rich God provides more than enough for us all to succeed. If our Biznistry has work it can't handle, we can send it to the business down the street. We can both be successful; our success doesn't mean their failure. This spiritual reality should undergird the principles set out in a Biznistry's business plan.

A business plan is essential, but it cannot predict changes and challenges that lie ahead. SSE Director Pete West tells new entrepreneurs to "expect seven problems. You won't know what they are until you start. If you expect difficulty, it will be easier to deal with it when it comes. You can't be discouraged by problems; you have to get through them." Pete says *the ability to adapt* is an important key to success.

In addition to adapting to problems and changes in the marketplace, a business plan must also be flexible enough to bend to God's leading as it is implemented. For example, the Amaizing Grace Kettle Corn Company's business plan called for a paid manager and hired workers to serve at the festival booth. When the anticipated startup funds did not materialize, the board decided instead to run solely on sweat equity—their own labor and that of volunteers. "We learned that this was what God wanted us to do," says Jim Mullaney, president of the Biznistry. "In hindsight I can see that if we had done it the way we laid out in the original business plan, I don't believe it would have worked. When you're following God's lead, even if by default, it works!"

For many individuals, churches, and charities, securing funding for a Biznistry can feel overwhelming. Many of us in ministry are already stretched financially just to cover day-to-day operating expenses, so investing in an enterprise that will take time to generate a return seems impossible. Individuals hesitate to put hard-earned savings at risk in a venture that has no guarantees. We've certainly experienced these frustrations ourselves.

The good news is that the Biznistry concept has an appeal that can attract investment dollars which might normally be elusive. Business people may get involved because they understand the long-term sustainability of the investment. Many organizations, like churches, can reduce costs by using facilities, equipment and even staffing that is already in place. Sometimes, individuals will self-fund the launch of a Biznistry because it represents an exciting new career direction for them.

All of these things have happened for us on the Grace Chapel Biznistry campus. A businessman in our congregation was intrigued by the idea of the thrift store, and made a significant financial investment in launching the first

New2You because he saw the long-term return it would generate for ministry. We use the facilities already available for Biznistry at Grace Chapel, and then pay rent which in turn benefits the church.

Mike Stretch launched Steadfast Studios, originally located on the Grace Chapel campus, funded by savings from the first half of his career. Certainly, using personal savings is a choice that should be made only after godly guidance and careful consideration of family needs. For Mike, who had years of experience in the graphic design field and a client base, it was a viable choice. He has since merged his design skills with the more technical marketing skills of another company to create Branding Ground, bringing a broader variety of skills and experience under one larger roof.

Gary Dawson started ReUse Centers with little but practical skills, sweat equity, and a creative idea for acquiring a building. At age 55, Gary was recovering from the recent failure of his own company and was looking for a new business opportunity. Falling back on his former trade as a pipe fitter, Gary was examining the sprinkler system in an old manufacturing building. A large, open building in an area of town no longer suited to manufacturing, it was little more than a dinosaur around the owner's neck. But Gary saw potential. Without funds to buy the building, Gary came up with a creative proposal—he would take over the building, rehab it, and generate income through rents. "We started with sweat equity to make the building into something that could be productive," explains Gary. "I had in mind a contractor's hub. I knew I could do that; I had done it before." He rehabbed the dinosaur and created spaces to rent out to small businesses. Five years later, Gary reports, "It now has a good income."

There are also traditional means of generating funds. One option is to build Biznistry into a fund-raising campaign. At Grace Chapel, this happened naturally as part of our capital campaign. We were *Building on Purpose* to finish out the multi-building campus, complete with Biznistries that would help fund the full scope of our ministry vision. Profits from the Biznistries flow directly to Self Sustaining Enterprises, a company separate from the church with its own board of directors and staff.

Another option is to borrow money, with the commitment to repay the debt through revenues. Responsible borrowing requires careful planning. A credit line from a bank may need to be personally secured, and being realistic about monetary need will help avoid problems later. Borrowing can be a viable option, although we must approach debt very cautiously as "the borrower is servant to the lender" (Proverbs 22:7). Start-up funding for ThriftSmart's first two stores, for example, came from individuals who were the largest benefactors of the four existing charities the stores were going to support. Because ThriftSmart didn't want to hurt the regular current funding of the charities, the $600,000 initial capital was collected through five-year notes at 6% interest. Although this capital was easily obtained, ThriftSmart CEO Dick Gygi no longer encourages this type of funding. His concern is that the stores now have to carry a debt, and revenues that could go to ministry are going to pay interest.

A third option is investment capital. It takes a special investor to back the Biznistry concept. Imagine telling an investment capitalist that not only will he be putting his money at risk, betting on an unproven management team and an idea, and waiting perhaps several years for a return (things a traditional investor is accustomed to accepting), but also that his personal return will be zero, because profits will flow through the company to charity. The investment return for Biznistry is not money, but the privilege and joy of seeing changed lives. Clearly, a Biznistry investor must be as committed to the cause as the leaders of the new company.

Some looking at Biznistry may wonder about selling shares in the enterprise to obtain capital from a larger pool of smaller investors. Although this is a standard means of obtaining start-up funds in traditional business, we discourage this for Biznistries, because the underlying premise of private ownership undermines the principle of Christian stewardship. No longer would the Biznistry have one owner (God) and one goal, but competing owners and agendas. Biznistries must reject any practice that would lead it to "serve two masters," for its resources belong only to God.

Grant or government funds may be another option. But again, beware; backers not committed to Biznistry principles may tempt or even require compromise. The city of Covington, Kentucky, for example, is impressed with Reset Ministry's success with helping ex-prisoners lead productive lives. But Gary Dawson, president of ReUse Centers that support the ministry, says he would never accept funds from the city, or federal or state funds either, even if they were offered. Why? "Strings," says Gary. "They always have strings attached. If I can't tell these guys [ex-prisoners] it's about turning their life over to Jesus, then I'm wasting my time, and I have no desire to do it."

However, the Biznistry does partner with the city of Covington in ways that can't compromise its mission. First, the ReUse Center gets many of its renovation materials free of charge through an arrangement with the city. When an old building is to be torn down, the city calls the Biznistry so they can salvage any reusable materials. Chandeliers and antique doors that would have been destined for a landfill now are featured, hard-to-find items for sale at the ReUse Center. The city's support also extends to Urban Partnership, affiliated with the ReUse Center, through a contract to pick up litter, clean graffiti, and remove weeds. The work provides jobs and income for the men in Reset ministries.

These business associations with the city advance the ministry of Reset without compromising its principles.

Converting Your Own Company: the SKILLSOURCE Example

Existing enterprises generally have little out-of-pocket cost associated with conversion to a Biznistry format. It's time, rather than money, that these enterprises invest, as they identify and pursue innovative ways to provide ministry while operating, and specify a ministry need that will become the recipient of their free cash flow.

When Skillsource converted to a Biznistry in 2004, its available resources began to sustain the faith-at-work ministry of At Work on Purpose. But this was only one result of the transformation that placed Christ at the heart of an already successful business. To gain an understanding of how a Biznistry honors and reflects God in the workplace, let's take a tour of an unusual office building.

The Green House is part of the ministry campus of Grace Chapel in Mason, Ohio. Once owned by a manufacturing company, the small house constructed in 1923 was only an empty shell when the church purchased the property—no plumbing, no furnace, no appliances. A church member rehabbed it so he and his family could live in it temporarily, and a couple of years later another church member converted it to office space for his design company.

When the house was again vacated, Chuck Proudfit saw the location as an ideal place to exemplify faith-based business, and Skillsource moved in—a successful, profit-making enterprise intentionally placed in the heart of town, right next door to a thrift store on a ministry campus. A 90-year-old two-story house of only 960 square feet was hardly the conventional idea of modern office space, but it has become an example of one of Biznistry's tenets: maximize use of available resources for greatest Kindgom impact.

After parking out front, we walk up the steps to the porch, and stop next to the inviting swing and rocking chair to ring the doorbell. We're welcomed by one of the staff, and step in to the small living room. Here we can plop onto the couch and share a cup of coffee while chatting in a comfortable, casual environment. Here we get the message that this business puts people and relationships first, and Skillsource wants to get to know us better. This place means business, but it feels like home.

Laura Jackson remembers the first time she stepped into that room after being hired at Skillsource: "It was pouring rain, and I had those first-day jitters. I work with rescue dogs a lot. They cower because of their past experiences, and react to any new situation by being fearful. I think I walked through the door like that. The only one there when I arrived was Melinda [Rea, Marketing Director]. The first thing she said to me was, 'It's OK. You're home.' Invoking those words of home and hearth made it a comforting and secure place."

A Biznistry places people first. Whether employees or clients, we strive to make them feel valued and welcomed. One Skillsource client liked the entrance room in the Green House so well he asked if it was available to rent out for business functions.

Just a few steps toward the rear of the house is the Strategy Room, the former kitchen/dining area. It includes some flexible workspace on the left and a large table on the right. The table is a gathering area, used for everything from meetings to prayer to lunch. The entire wall behind the table is painted glossy white, creating a giant whiteboard that gets lots of use for brainstorming and planning. This table, where both employees and clients can meet, represents more of what is different about Biznistry.

First, a Biznistry sees itself as the body of Christ, where each member is valued for serving an important function. "We're not only here to work together, we're here to affirm each other," says Melinda. "That's a real distinction between our company and other companies."

Laura explains: "I've worked in a number of different work environments, some more toxic than others, some good. But when I came here, it was different the minute I walked in the door. It comes down to personal worth. Often when you're in a company, large or small, you feel replaceable. It's maybe a byproduct of the Industrial

Revolution. I'm on a line, working this little section; but if something should happen to me tomorrow they could find another minion to fill my place. That pervades our work environment in general in the U.S. Why would I affirm a coworker? That might diminish my role; maybe I'm replaceable. People become competitive, instead of cooperative."

Here at the table, ideas are shared, and employees work together as a team, encouraging and helping each other. "We're very open about the fact that we love each other," says Melinda. "We love working together, and we love what we do. That love we have from God we bring to each other, each and every day. It sounds kind of mushy," she admits, "but it's true."

"It's not that we don't have difficult conversations," adds Marcene Nichols, a marketing strategist. "We keep each other accountable, and give constructive criticism. It's just that we see this as a safe place, and if someone gives criticism, we know it's done in love."

The women agree that the basis of their work relationship is the respect and trust that Chuck has fostered as a leader. "He's very intentional and consistent about it," says Marcene. "He's intentional about the people who are brought in as employees—if you're not willing to work in a place where you have to take a sacrificial approach to things, you might not be a good fit."

The table is also where the Bible and prayer meet life at work. It's the place the staff meets every Tuesday for "Lunch and Learn," a flexible discussion time led by Melinda, ranging from discussion of a Sunday sermon or Bible verse to business challenges and politics. The talk is a mix of business and personal, always focusing on living out faith in the real world and always including prayer. "Other companies have prayer groups," Melinda acknowledges, "but for us, it's as much a part of who we are and what we do as ordering supplies every month."

Prayer at Skillsource is both planned and spontaneous. Every week Laura collects prayer requests and answers to past prayers, and distributes them to the staff by email. It's a way to be intentional but also authentic about connecting and supporting each other and the company. Sometimes a staff member comes in with a need and asks for prayer. Then all work stops, and everyone takes time to pray about the situation. "It's just woven into life," explains Laura.

This lower level of the Green House is the incubator, where relationships, ideas, and planning grow. It doesn't just happen Monday through Friday. On weekends, Chuck makes the space available to Jobs Plus, a ministry focusing on job readiness training, job placement and mentoring. The ministry has opened an office in the New2You building next door, and the Green House offers Jobs Plus clients and counselors a private area for interviews and one-on-one coaching. Opening the doors to Jobs Plus is one way of using business resources to promote marketplace ministry.

Next we walk up the stairs to the second floor. Here is where strategy and brainstorming are translated into practical application. Each staff member has a desk here on the upper floor, but you won't find them all here from nine to five. When Chuck transformed Skillsource into a Biznistry, he was committed to putting people first by giving employment to some who may not fit the traditional concept.

Rather than relying on an application and a short interview or two, Chuck spent time getting to know each of his employees before they were hired. He considered their gifts, skills, experiences, and personal situations for how they fit the Biznistry model, and prayed for God's leading. Those he chose for his staff reflect a difference in hiring philosophy between traditional business and Biznistry.

Melinda, for example, had been laid off in her early 60s, with virtually no prospects for new full-time employment in the marketing field despite her years of experience in a number of different industries. Marcene, with school-age children at home, also had much to offer, but she had been out of the workforce for nine years being a full-time mom, and now she needed part-time employment. Chuck created the Marketing Matters division of Skillsource, although it was not part of his original core concept for the company, to allow Melinda and Marcene to contribute their skills, experience, and passion for service to his clients.

Laura is single with four children and five grandchildren. Her story of employment at Skillsource exemplifies the heart of Biznistry: "I have gone through some personal challenges in my life which left me not being the best version of myself, and I started here in that state. And I thought I must be out of my mind—you don't come to a company at a weak point; you bring all your strengths. Nobody wants to give the perception that they're weak; that's not how it works in business. So it was really challenging for me coming at a point when I wasn't at my best.

"During my first couple of weeks, Chuck commented to me, 'I knew you were exhausted when I hired you.' I thought, oh great, that's what I was projecting? You're wearing a suit, and you think you're projecting your best! So I said, 'Of all the people you had to choose from, you thought, Let's go with the exhausted one?' But Chuck replied, 'No. What I saw was your potential, and who you were. I wasn't looking at your circumstances right at that moment—I was looking at you as a person. And I feel it's my role, and the company's role, to come alongside you and help you to reach your potential, whatever that takes. The ship isn't sailing without you. As long as it takes, you're still on board.'"

Biznistry is not only committed to discipling employees in the workplace, but is also intentional in seeking ministry opportunities, even in hiring, while growing its business.

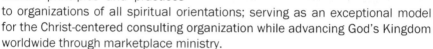

PASSION

Leading a global effort to bring biblical principles and practices to organizations of all spiritual orientations; serving as an exceptional model for the Christ-centered consulting organization while advancing God's Kingdom worldwide through marketplace ministry.

PURPOSE

To unleash the Organization, revealing purpose beyond profit to realize the full potential of organizations in the marketplace. Originally providing revenue to start At Work On Purpose, SKILLSOURCE generates profits that are also reinvested in strategic marketplace ministry initiatives worldwide.

PLAN

Build a consulting model that reaches expertly across industries and geographies. Deliver sustainable growth in sales, profits and people to client companies through Accelerated Corporate Evolution (ACE™). Funnel all available profits to marketplace ministry initiatives.

> "Fulfilling God's purpose for our work is an important part of fulfilling God's purpose for our life."
>
> Chuck Proudfit, founder & CEO

PRACTICE

Staff: Originally a one-person consultancy, SKILLSOURCE now has staff specialists in strategy, marketing, sales and operations, while also continuing to contract with a wide range of specialists in additional areas such as finance, public relations, and internet presence.

Finances: Converting from a traditional business minimized startup costs. After 10 years as a Biznistry, Skillsource has donated an average of $10,000+ per year in profits released for marketplace ministry initiatives.

Keys to Success:

- Discerning God's path and pace for the organization, and then following God's lead in designing and deploying growth plans
- Delivering consistent excellence for clients, while adapting to their changing needs
- Maintaining a debt-free financial position
- Cultivating visibility in the marketplace with earned awards for excellence

The newest Skillsource employee, Michelle Thompson, says Chuck's leadership is based on his trust that God has sent the right people to Skillsource. "An important part of being a great leader is knowing that you can't be into every little thing; you have to trust that the people on the team God sent you will get the job done. Chuck has shown great faith in that, and he reaffirms that in us."

This faith that God will guide his workers creates a foundation of respect and trust that flows through Chuck to his staff. It is demonstrated daily in small things like employees having the freedom to take time off when needed for personal appointments or needs. "In another business, you have to schedule time off for a doctor's appointment," explains Melinda. "Here we know what we have to do. We have to serve our clients, and we are trusted to get it done. That's a huge distinction. There are companies even in today's world that want to see you slogging away from 8 until 5 so they know you're doing your work." Trust shows that an employer values his staff, and it reflects the godly priority of putting people first.

We've got one more room to visit in this little house. You get to it by pulling down a ladder from the hallway ceiling. At the top of the ladder you climb into the Dream Room, snuggled under the roof. The slanted roof is too low for us to stand up, but that's okay, because this is a room for relaxing, tipping your head back, and looking into the blue sky and clouds painted on the ceiling. There's carpet, heat and air conditioning, music, and comfy bean bag chairs and a low table. This room is made to be a vacation for those who can't get away, a place to dream for those who haven't dreamed in years. It's a creative use of an otherwise unused resource, intended for anyone needing to get away, but especially for the Jobs Plus clients. Many of these men and women have been merely surviving day to day; taking time to get alone with God in the Dream Room helps them set goals and plan for a brighter future. It's also a place of hope, a reminder that God "can do immeasurably more than all we ask or imagine."[18]

It's clear that people are growing in this Green House. But there's another reason for its name: it will soon become the first Net Zero Energy building in Mason. The building will serve as an inspiring, concrete example of sustainability, an important Biznistry tenet.

Maybe you think what's happening at Skillsource sounds too good to be true. You wouldn't be alone. Laura Jackson interacts with many different people in her professional and personal life, so she often has opportunities to tell both Christians and non-Christians about her experience at work. "I always get the same reaction," she says. "They just look at me, with mouth open, like, 'You've got to be kidding me.' I've actually had several people say, 'That's not the way business works.' Well, it can. It does. Because it *is* working."

The Skillsource staff is passionate about marketplace ministry, and hope to set an example of what God can do when we live out our faith through our work. "No company is going to be like ours, and yet each company has its own mission, its own value," says Laura. "We want to at least introduce the idea of operating this way, and let each company flesh it out however it fits their culture. But I really believe that business can and should be done this way. I don't think it should be the exception, and I'd love to see it be the rule."

Visitors to the Green House see a healthy Biznistry in action. What they cannot easily see is the lives that have been changed all over the world because of the hundreds of thousands of dollars Skillsource has contributed to marketplace ministry in all its forms. Providing a regular, sustainable source of funding for ministry is one of the primary purposes of Biznistry, and this goal requires a great deal of soul-searching and planning. When Chuck converted his successful, mostly one-person consulting business to a Biznistry, he took a careful look at his own salary. Because of his commitment to support At Work On Purpose and other marketplace ministry initiatives, he decided to limit his salary to an amount acceptable for the kind of work he does, but far less than he would be capable of earning elsewhere. Here is where the heart meets the head—where each Biznistry leader or board must prayerfully seek God's perspective in allocating salary and ministry funds, recognizing their high calling to be stewards of what belongs only to God.

Creative Solutions and God Moments

As any Biznistry calculates its operating costs, it may want to consider some cost-cutting strategies that are common in ministry but uncommon in a traditional business. For example, using volunteers for some tasks in the Biznistry not only saves money, but also provides a variety of ministry opportunities not normally offered by the local church. Amaizing Grace Kettle Corn's all-volunteer staff, coordinated by a committed board of directors from the church whose ministries it supports, allows the Biznistry to maximize its profits that help fund the church's community outreach. One Bistro, Chef Robert Adamson's community café, also uses volunteers for all restaurant tasks besides cooking. Volunteers are glad to help because they are directly ministering to people in need.

Because our God is creative, Biznistries may find unexpected help through what Biznistry owner Dave Stacy calls "God Moments." When Dave and his wife Amber needed repairs to the elaborate coffee-brewing machine that had come with the kiosk they were renovating to open Sunrise Coffee, they called the manufacturer, who quoted a price well beyond the Biznistry's means. When they called the subcontractor who would have been assigned the job, they discovered he lived nearby and ran a coffee-roasting business. He offered to fix the expensive brewing machine free of charge to gain Sunrise Coffee as a customer for his locally-roasted coffee beans. Biznistries are full of God Moments, because the people who lead them rely on God's guidance and supply, which he promises to give as we follow his plan.

A Biznistry may also find unexpected help from a traditional Better Business that wants to be seen as an asset to its community and recognizes the Biznistry as an efficient and reliable means of distributing its support. Its help may come from donations of in-kind goods and services, or resources provided at a reduced cost. For example, as our New2You thrift store building was being renovated, the owner of a local concrete company poured a large area of concrete flooring at or below cost. He sacrificed his profit because he wanted to impact the lives of needy children.

Another kind of unexpected help may come when word about an innovative Biznistry attracts interest and publicity. This happened with our Aquaponics venture. After creating and testing a combined fish and vegetable growing system to be replicated in a Nigerian village, Self Sustaining Enterprises looked for ways to use the technology here at home to bring fresh, nutritious food to urban pockets of need. The project attracted the attention of Krohn Conservatory in Cincinnati, which invited SSE to build and display an aquaponics system at their location as part of a short-term educational exhibit.

Word then traveled to the Cincinnati Zoo & Botanical Gardens, where SSE helped install an aquaponics system that provides food for the zoo restaurant, named in 2013 the greenest restaurant in the U.S. Although SSE did not profit financially from these initiatives, the publicity and education they provide helps promote the mission of SSE and may lead to other resources. The projects have also provided hands-on learning opportunities for high school students, perhaps inspiring them to find their own innovative responses to poverty.

As your Biznistry develops, you will find ways to expand your business and ministry, sometimes in ways not foreseen when you made your business model. But you will use your model to examine additions and changes to be sure they are consistent with the foundational purposes and procedures you so carefully researched and spelled out in the beginning. Your model will also be helpful in guiding the difficult decisions you will inevitably have to make.

This is simply an overview of the kind of plans and principles that form the foundation of Biznistries. We can help with these and much more, and we want you to learn from our experience, so please contact us. You'll find a list of resources at the end of this book.

Notes

[1] Amanda Webber, "Profitability Measurement for a New Business," Startup Nation <www.startupnation.com> ; Small Business Administration, http://www.sba.gov/sites/default/files/sbfaq.pdf

[2] Matthew 10:16

[3] Nehemiah 1:3

[4] Nehemiah 1:4

[5] Nehemiah 2:2

[6] Nehemiah 1:4-11

[7] Nehemiah 2:5-8

[8] Nehemiah 2:11-3:32

[9] Nehemiah 2:18

[10] Nehemiah 4:6-10

[11] Nehemiah 4:14-18

[12] Nehemiah 5:1-9

[13] Nehemiah 5:10-18

[14] see Proverbs 15:22

[15] see Job 1

[16] see James 1:2-4

[17] see Romans 12:1-2

[18] Ephesians 3:20

5

Biznistry and the Church

Let's not go to church. Let's be the church. –Bridget Willard

Why would a church get involved with Biznistry? The most obvious reason is to provide additional funding to realize its vision. The church has limited resources, and Biznistry gives the body of Christ a way to extend beyond the boundaries of the general giving to further fund existing missions, or to fund new ministry opportunities.

As well as providing supplemental revenue, Biznistry can also help the local church be a better steward of the resources it already has. In Jesus' Parable of the Talents, the servant who safely hid the money entrusted to him and returned it later was called wicked, lazy and worthless.[1] The master expected his servants to steward his money shrewdly, putting it to work to achieve the maximum increase. God expects no less of his church.

God provides enough money through his people for the work of the church, and church leaders generally understand the importance of thrift and using resources wisely. But sometimes when leaders lack the practical skills to handle the congregation's tithes and offerings efficiently, distribution comes up short. Because Biznistry embraces the best practices of both ministry and business, its principles and training help church leaders make the wise financial decisions that can fully fund God's work and earn the Master's approval.

Church finances are important. We all agree, however, that the church is about a lot more than money. A church strategy to bring in more money is pointless—and, more importantly, Godless—if it departs from God's plan for the body of Christ. Let's look beyond funding to discover how Biznistry fulfills, rather than compromises, the mission of the church.

Who's the Minister?

The church, of course, is not a building. It is people—people who follow Christ. The Bible says the church is Christ's body, made up of many different parts but united by his Spirit. The church, according to 1 Corinthians 12 and Ephesians 4, is God's hands, feet, eyes, and mouth in the world, and each believer is important in the functioning of the whole. God's purpose for his body is summed up in the Great Commandment and the Great Commission: we are to love God with all our heart, soul, and mind, and love our neighbor as ourselves,[2] and we are to go into the world and make disciples of all nations.[3] Simply put, the church is Jesus' physical presence in the world today, and it is to be doing all the things Jesus would do if he were still here physically on earth.

We have seen that Christ's earthly ministry was not confined to a building or a particular day of the week. Most of his public appearances were in the marketplace; most of his parables are in a non-church setting; and he chose his closest followers from outside the clergy. When God raised Jesus from the dead, he seated him at his right hand in heaven, and made him head of the church—but that's not all:

> And God placed *all things* under his feet and appointed him to be head over *everything* for the church, which is his body, the fullness of him who fills *everything* in *every way*.[4]

God intended the church to use *all* the resources of the world he created. And just as Christ's earthly ministry and his heavenly authority is evident in every aspect of life, so his church is to be his heart, hands, and feet at home, at work, at school, and in the marketplace.

Most would agree the church has fallen woefully short of this calling. We have seen how the ancient Greek concept of dualism has permeated our Western culture, conditioning us to separate the sacred and the secular, our faith and our work. This divide is not just cultural—it has invaded the church as well. The church has little presence in the marketplace, and is hesitant about embracing "worldly" business practices it fears may bring compromise and corruption. A local church may even pride itself on being a sacred haven of the soul, separate from the material world. Ministry is done mostly by paid professionals. The vast majority of believers not in "full-time Christian service" live outside the spiritual realm, contributing to "God's work" by giving money and a bit of spare time to support the church's staff and programs.

Contrast this dualistic view with the early church, described in the book of Acts. Local churches were groups of believers meeting in homes or outdoors. They were active in the marketplace: Lydia, whose house was used for meetings, was a "dealer in purple cloth"[5]; Aquila, Priscilla, and even the apostle Paul worked making tents at the same time they ministered.[6] The Bible mentions no paid professional ministers. In fact, early believers did not passively listen to sermons—they interacted with each other. Paul instructs the Corinthian church: "When you come together, everyone has a hymn, or a word of instruction, a revelation, a tongue or an interpretation. All of these must be done for the strengthening of the church."[7]

This is not to say there is anything wrong with a church having paid pastors. The problem comes when we accept the dualistic lay/clergy division, effectively relegating believers working in the marketplace to second-class status. This view is counter to the Bible's description of the church as a body made up of many different and equally important parts. Jesus appointed some to be pastors and teachers,[8] but not all. Every believer is uniquely gifted to serve God in the church, and every kind of God-given gift is needed to represent the fullness of Christ. The church "grows and builds itself up in love" only "as each part does its work."[9]

Yet the great divide between secular and sacred has convinced marketplace Christians that because they are not paid professionals, they can't do ministry. Their spiritual purpose at work, if they have one, is to make money and give some of it to the church. They are not ministers, but they can pay a minister or refer someone to a minister. In effect, they are paying the church to perform ministry in their place, thus abdicating their responsibility as Christians.

Pastor Jeff Greer is passionate about this, but he says it's not the fault of the congregation; church members are simply doing what they've been taught to do: "I believe we pastors have facilitated this distorted view of ministry by failing to fulfill our biblical responsibility. My job as a pastor is not to minister *on behalf* of my congregation, but to *equip believers* to do the works of ministry. Paul says some members of the body have been given the gifts of teaching and evangelism 'to prepare God's people for works of service' so that each part of Christ's body, the church, may attain 'the whole measure of the fullness of Christ.'[9] In other words, the church cannot fully become what God has planned for it to be unless each believer is actively involved in the works of service God has prepared for us to do.

"All believers belong to God, no matter where they are or what they are doing. Paul says, 'If we live, we live to the Lord; and if we die, we die to the Lord. So, whether we live or die, we belong to the Lord.'[10] "Living" here doesn't mean just at church. You don't belong to your job, or to the world; you belong to God. Living to the Lord means all you do—at church, at home, at work—is to be ministry to God. I as a pastor should know better than to take your check and do your job. Yes, God wants you to give financially to the church, and some of those funds free up pastors to fulfill their purpose—but not to do your ministry for you. My job is to *equip you* to minister and to send you back into the world and the workplace with a purpose."

As we have seen, many Christians have heard a voice deep inside telling them they were made for more than making money for ministry—they are meant to minister. As a businessman with a big heart for ministry, Chuck Proudfit has often heard other Christians in the marketplace say, "I've thought about leaving my job to go into ministry." Let's look deeper—what are they really saying? "I'm not in ministry where I am, and if pastors like Jeff are professionals in ministry, then I'm unprofessional." Churches have failed to give their people a vision beyond provision. The body of believers, the church, is gathered on Sunday; let's devote some of that time to equip them for ministry as they scatter into the world on Monday.

Supporting the Purposes of the Church

Equipping the saints for ministry is called Discipleship, and it's one of the foundational church purposes based in the Great Commandment and the Great Commission. As we examine each of these purposes, we'll see that Biznistry not only breaks down the sacred/secular wall, but also builds on the church's foundation.

Worship

God intended work to be worship. In fact, the Old Testament uses the same word, *avodah*, for both "work" and "worship." In the New Testament, Paul explains two purposes God has for our work when he tells the Thessalonians, "Make it your ambition to lead a quiet life, to mind your own business and *to work with your hands*, just as we told you, so that your daily life may win the respect of outsiders and so that you will not be dependent on anybody."[11] God is with us as we work, and work done for him, whatever that may be, brings him glory.

Church members involved in Biznistry see worship as more than an hour experience on Sunday mornings. Their skills are used to worship God. Marketing becomes worship, sales becomes worship, manual labor becomes worship, finance becomes worship—because the work is centered on God. Psalms 24:1 says, "The earth is the Lord's and everything in it, the world, and all who live in it." Biznistry workers begin to realize that everything they have, everything they are, belongs to God, and as they work they are giving it all back to him in worship. When you hear people say things like, "I'm no longer a wealth builder; now I'm a Kingdom builder," you can begin to understand the transformation. They realize they exist to worship him.

Evangelism

How Christians live and love has an impact on those watching. What does it say to the world when we don't care for those in need in our own community? When we allow people in developing countries to starve to death, to die of easily treatable diseases, or to go without clean water, proper education, and adequate clothing? Look at the example of the early New Testament church—they shared their resources. They eliminated poverty within their realm of influence, and "the Lord added to their number daily those who were being saved."[12]

The church shows Christ to the world by displaying love within and outside the body of Christ. This is true evangelism. And Biznistry is one way of creating opportunities to share the gospel and explain "the reason for the hope that you have"[13] and why we are different.

What does evangelism look like in your church and community? If you're like most Christians, you probably think of people knocking on door after door, hoping to find someone home who won't be too annoyed to listen to a gospel message or accept a tract. Or perhaps you think of a special church-sponsored program aimed at the unsaved, with frequent reminders to church members to invite their friends. There's nothing wrong with either of these approaches. But are they the best ways to reach people with the gospel?

Think about where people spend their time, and you'll discover the greatest evangelistic opportunities. Most adults spend a large chunk of their waking hours at work, making the marketplace a huge, mostly untouched mission field. Most good pastors would love the opportunity to be able to reach out to people in the work world and share the love of Christ, but that doesn't often happen.

Biznistry has given Pastor Jeff opportunities to connect with men and women he would not have had a chance to know otherwise. "I've talked with CEOs of large companies, scientists, business leaders in our community, and to organizations such as the Rotary Club," explains Jeff. "I can empathize with the difficulties they face in the work world because I, too, have experienced financial setbacks, staff problems, and legal dilemmas. I'm passionate about their concerns because they are also my concerns, and this has earned me their trust and respect. The divide goes down because I've left my 'sacred' world and gone into their 'secular' world.

"I've also found that our church's involvement with Biznistry has given me a built-in conversation starter when new people come in to the church. I ask, 'What do you do?', and no matter how they respond, I'm able to make them feel their skills are useful and needed at the church. I may even be able to connect them with one of our Biznistries.

"So Biznistry has given me, a pastor, new opportunities to reach people for Christ. But I still cannot just walk into any place of business and expect to have an audience for the gospel. Jesus called all believers, not just pastors, to be his witnesses—and for very good reason. Each of us has his or her own sphere of influence, and each of us is needed to represent Jesus to the world."

Practically speaking, how do Christians share their faith in the world outside the church? Traditional methods of evangelism have little success in our modern culture. Most people aren't home during working hours, and don't want to be bothered by strangers at the door when they are home. Evangelistic events require churches to figure out some way to get people who come to church to get other people to come to church to hear a gospel message; in effect, we're asking unbelievers to come to us. Certainly believers should be encouraged to invite their friends to church. But Jesus commissioned us to GO into all the world and make disciples.[14] "All the world" includes school, home, and work.

The simplest and most effective way to reach the world of work is for each member of Christ's body to go where he is already going, day after day, and reach out to the lost people he or she finds there. Most of us working in the marketplace don't know how to do this. We're not even sure we *want* to do this. The problem is not that we lack a mission field; the problem is that we don't know how to be missionaries. The church doesn't have a crisis of evangelism; it has a crisis of discipleship. So in order to better understand how Biznistry builds evangelism, let's look more closely at how it develops discipleship.

Discipleship

Jesus' Great Commission gives the church the responsibility of making disciples, teaching and leading believers to grow in their relationship to God and to become more like his Son. Sunday morning worship, teaching, and fellowship certainly help guide believers toward this goal, but an hour or two out of 168 isn't enough. If the body of Christ is to fully realize its purpose in equipping believers to be missionaries every day of the week, wherever they are, it needs areas of involvement outside the walls of its building.

Jerry's pastor had occasionally admonished the congregation, "Whatever you do, work at it with all your heart, as working for the Lord, not for men,"[15] but somehow, those words had always stayed in the pews when Jerry and his church family left the building on Sunday. A local church actively involved in Biznistry can provide members like Jerry with real-life opportunities in work that is *intentionally purposed* for ministry. Biznistry provides the discipleship to support the teaching.

Biznistry allows a pastor to teach the word and apply the word. Information plus application equals transformation, and Biznistry is a great tool for discipleship because it consistently provides the practice to go along with the preaching. When the bottom line of a business is ministry, workers in that business must continually examine how well they are serving as Jesus' hands and feet. Are they using their God-given gifts to their fullest extent? Are they putting people above profit? Are they seeking the highest good of others rather than themselves? Biznistry offers daily opportunities for its workers to exhibit the very mind and heart of God.

Our Innovate group gives us an opportunity to disciple entrepreneurs in our church in a way we never thought possible. As they use their God-given gifts to build God's Kingdom, they grow. They see themselves as ministers, and as missionaries to the marketplace. The words of Deuteronomy 8:18 come alive: "But remember the Lord your God, for it is he who gives you the ability to produce wealth," and they realize the skills they have to make money belong to God. All their gifts, all their talents, and all their abilities belong to him and should be used to serve him. When they start to understand and own that concept, their lives are transformed. Their Christianity moves from Sunday mornings to 7/24/365.

As they see the lives of others changed, it builds their confidence in how God can use them to further the cause of Christ. Hearts awaken, passions ignite, and men and women are unleashed to be the people they were created to be. God has been taken out of his box and let loose on their lives, and they can't get enough. The stories of how God used the heroes of the Bible spark a flame in their hearts, and they want the same experience for themselves.

Pastor Jeff says his new experience in business has allowed him to minister to those in the marketplace from a whole new perspective. "I never truly understood the struggles, temptations, challenges, stresses, hardships and emotions that people who work in the marketplace every day have to endure until we started our Biznistries," Jeff says. "Now I understand (if even in a small way) the stress of a businessman on the brink of collapse, because I have faced the same thing with one of our thrift stores. I understand how difficult it is to keep your integrity when your employer is asking you to cut corners or to lie. I can speak to the heart of someone who has separated her work life from her Christian life. Recently a church member was relating his business situation, and interrupted himself for a moment. 'I love that I don't have to stop and explain all this to you,' he said, and then he continued. Those who work in the marketplace no longer feel I am removed from their experience; they know I understand because I walk in their world with them."

Ministry

The Parable of the Talents has shown us how God made his people stewards of the financial resources needed to perform his work in the world. The servants in the parable were expected to *use* the resources the master provided, not bury them for safety. Was Jesus speaking only of money here? Other biblical passages would suggest he was including *all* God-given resources. For example, Peter writes, "Each one should use whatever gift he has received to serve others, faithfully administering God's grace in its various forms."[16]

All of God's people have been given spiritual gifts and abilities, not just money. We see these gifts being exercised by faithful Sunday school teachers and choir directors. But what about the businessman who has a mind for marketing? Or the engineering consultant? Does the self-employed entrepreneur have gifts that can be used in the church?

Biznistry allows all believers to use their gifts and abilities, including business skills. It opens up avenues of service that most churches have never thought about, encouraging all Christians to be ministers. We've seen how the lack of financial management skills can affect how far a congregation's giving will stretch. When the church comes to recognize what it would call business skills as gifts that God has provided to some of his people for serving the body of

Christ, both the church and the individual benefit. For example, Jack, retired CFO of a large retail corporation, was recently inspired to volunteer his business expertise for both Self Sustaining Enterprises and for our church. We would not be able to pay him for his financial management work; he is motivated because he understands his unique skills are needed in the body of Christ, and his service is a ministry that advances the Kingdom of God.

Many pastors lament the lack of involvement of people in their congregations, particularly the men. At Grace Chapel, some men are now serving for the first time since we started our Biznistries. One is using his marketing and branding skills to better communicate our message and purpose to the community; another is using administrative skills to streamline day-to-day staffing of the various church ministries. The problem is not that people don't have a heart for ministry; it's that the church has failed to offer avenues of service that use all of its God-given resources. Biznistry is one way to provide new opportunities that build up both the believer and the body. It allows the church to lead in demonstrating the integrated synergy possible between business and ministry.

Amaizing Grace Kettle Corn Company, a Biznistry connected with a church and purposed to fund outreach in the local community, attracts thousands of people to its popcorn booth at festivals. To capitalize on this ministry opportunity, the company provides an evangelistic message on each bag and includes church information on its flyers. Volunteers from the congregation take samples of their quality product into the crowds, literally "going into the world" where they often discover opportunities for ministry to people they may never have touched otherwise. "We're not shy about saying we're a church," says Amaizing Grace president Jim Mullaney. When a man came to the booth with a cast on his leg, Jim asked him how it happened, and as their conversation ended he offered to add the man to his prayer list.

The Biznistry brings Christ's love not only to customers, but also to booth volunteers, and to the festival sponsors and organizers. "It's all about being as kind as we can be and as open as we can be," says Jim. The Amaizing Grace team continually prays for God to show them new ways to turn casual contact over a bag of popcorn into meaningful ministry.

Fellowship

What better way to develop a deep relationship with another believer than to work together on something you're both passionate about? Biznistry is inherently a team experience. It provides the dynamics of a small group, apart from the larger congregation, for people to get to know one another better. Relationships begin as believers work together on a business plan, and deepen as they face the challenges and joys of working side by side on a project.

Biznistry allows more people to be actively involved in the body of believers. Bob the sales rep used to dutifully tag along after his wife to a potluck supper, trying to remember names so he could greet people again on Sunday morning. Now he has found a place to use his skills in a retail-sales Biznistry, developing deeper relationships with people in his church and others in the Christian community. When he's having a tough time seeing God at work on a Tuesday, he's got a fellow believer at his side to encourage him. When a coworker is worried about her daughter's health problems, Bob is able to sit down for a moment and pray with her.

Pastor Valerie Waibel, part of the Amaizing Grace Kettle Corn Company team, says spending a day at a festival making and serving popcorn with other volunteers from her church gives her more opportunities to connect with congregation members in a relaxed way. She says that working together helps the volunteers develop fruits of the Spirit—especially patience, when lines are long and the booth is busy. "We pray together early in the day," says founder Jim Mullaney. "One day I prayed that we would all still be speaking to each other by the end of the day!" Sometimes there are quieter times, when workers can share family concerns and offer each other support.

The Amaizing Grace team has learned that God's direction to run the business with volunteers rather than the paid staff they first envisioned has brought unexpected benefits, especially the opportunity for fellowship and bringing together skills from many different people. Biznistry at its best is the body of Christ, the church, using all the resources that Christ has given her to be his mind, heart, hands and feet in not just the church building, but in the world.

One Church's Amaizing Grace

Before the Amaizing Grace Kettle Corn team enjoyed fellowship along with service in their Biznistry, they first had to face opposition. We share their story here because it is typical of the challenges met by those who introduce Biznistry to the local church.

Jim Mullaney was frustrated with church committees. As founder and CEO of his own company, he was used to action, and the church committees he had served on seemed to move as slowly as a snail in molasses. But he had a vision for his church: a Ministry Campus focused on reaching beyond internal church work to their community, much of it economically depressed. His excitement for Biznistry fueled his passion, and he acted.

"I drew up a schematic of a building that outlined my vision," explains Jim. "In that building were several rooms: a youth ministry, a music ministry, our existing preschool, congregational care, evangelism, and a Biznistry to help fund these operations." Jim showed his drawing to Greg, a friend on the church's mission committee, and Greg asked for a write-up to present to a vision team on the committee. Twice Greg told him he would be asked to make a presentation to the committee—but the invitation never materialized. "Your idea is too far out of the box; we just can't get our hands on it," someone told Jim. "But that Biznistry thing seems a bit intriguing."

Jim says, "When the third person came up to me and said that, I thought 'the door's open a crack.'" Firmly placing his foot in that crack, Jim asked Pastor Valerie Waibel and five other church members to join him in setting up an ad-hoc committee to investigate possibilities for a Biznistry. After deciding the idea was feasible, they identified 31 potential business ideas in a brainstorming session. Then they examined each idea, looking for the one that would generate the most profit for the least amount of work. Eventually they settled on Kettle Corn, a sweet-and-salty premium popcorn they could sell at festivals and other gatherings. An Ohio company would supply all the equipment, ingredients, and instruction they would need for $9,000.

The committee figured they would need $15,000 in start-up costs to launch the Biznistry. "Our thinking was, that's no problem; we've got lots of members in the church," remembers Jim. "We'll have no problem getting members to contribute as soon as they find out what this is all about." They developed a business plan, and Jim and Val made up a list of some prominent members of the congregation who might be able to back them financially. The committee invited these members to a series of breakfasts where they presented the Biznistry plan. And that's when the sparks began to fly.

"We'd be like money-changers in the temple," some said (although no sales would be conducted in the church). "It's like Catholic festivals, and we don't want to get involved in that," said another. Another feared that members would no longer tithe if money was coming in through a business. In the end, two of the invited members contributed $1500 each. Instead of $15,000, the committee ended up with only $3,000. The committee decided the church was not comfortable with the Biznistry idea.

Pastor Val, supportive of the Biznistry vision from the beginning, encouraged church members to join the team and give the enterprise a chance. She says the Biznistry adds support to the church's vision: *Win* people to Christ, *Equip* them to minister, and *Send* them into the community and the world. "A lot of churches across the country have fundraisers; they have something on-site at the church and expect people to come to them," she says. "We've been doing it that way a long time, but the world's changed. I think we've got to go out to them, and not be afraid to do that."

Carl Icahn, the billionaire investor and entrepreneur, once said, "In life and business, there are two cardinal sins. The first is to act precipitously without thought, and the second is not to act at all." Although their idea did not get the reception they desired, the committee was convinced the vision for funding church ministry was a workable plan given them by God and they opted to act. Jim asked Chuck Proudfit, who had inspired his idea for church Biznistry, to meet with the committee. Chuck suggested they could ease the anxiety of church members by setting up their Biznistry as a non-profit organization separate from the church. This strategy made sense, and Jim submitted to the "brutal" process of obtaining 501(c)(3) certification from the state of Ohio.

For the funding, Jim says, "We decided to just make it happen." The committee members pooled personal funds and came up with just enough to buy the needed equipment. To prepare for the festivals, Jim says, "We figured we'll just go out on a limb, buy the product on our credit card, pray it doesn't rain, and see if we can make it work." In its first six months Amaizing Grace Kettle Corn Company's all-volunteer staff had made $13,000 in sales, and with 85% of that being profit, the Biznistry was already established and ready to disburse funds.

When the time finally came to present the new enterprise to the church's leadership team, the decision was not whether they should proceed with the plan; that was already done, and the Biznistry was functioning as a non-profit separate from the church. The only decision the church leaders had to make was if they wanted to accept the profits for church missions.

Amaizing Grace Kettle Corn

PASSION

Church members see great need in their community and want to reach out in the name of Jesus.

PURPOSE

Provide financial support for community outreach programs of Lindenwald United Methodist Church in Hamilton, Ohio, and other local ministries.

PLAN

The founding board chose Kettle Corn because it provided one-source training, equipment, and product as well as a high profit margin. The premium popcorn is prepared with portable equipment and sold at a variety of festivals and events. With a home base on the Lindenwald Ministry Campus, the enterprise is a separate 501(c)(3) organization.

PRACTICE

Staff: All volunteers, consisting of a founding board and other short-term workers

Finances: When the original plan for the enterprise to be part of the church met opposition and fundraising from church donors came up short, the board invested their own money to purchase the needed equipment and became certified as a nonprofit organization.

> "So many endeavors have been locked out at church. When we started this enterprise, the congregation said, 'What's going on here? This thing's moving!'"
>
> Jim Mullaney, founder

Keys to Success:

- Low initial costs and instruction provided by the Kettle Corn supplier simplified start-up
- All-volunteer staff and high profit margin enabled profits the first year
- Affiliation with a local church facilitates conversation at community events, while separate legal status respects diversity of views in the congregation
- Enterprise has full support and participation of the church's pastor

The planning and implementation of the Biznistry was something new for the church, where, as in most churches, committees often stagnate. "So many endeavors have been locked out at church," Jim observes. "When we started this Biznistry, we launched it real quick, and it shocked the congregation—in a good way. 'What's going on here? This thing's moving!' people said."

"A lot of things get bogged down in committee," Pastor Val agrees. "They want to have ownership and control, but God has the ownership and control."

Jim believes the business and cultural environment in the world today doesn't allow the luxury of lengthy deliberation and review. He hopes Amaizing Grace may serve as an example that will bring life and action to other committees, but he's not overly optimistic. Change at church doesn't come easily.

So far, Amaizing Grace Kettle Corn has given all of its profits to their church's mission endeavors, but they may begin to support other ministries as well. Jim says the beauty of the church/Biznistry relationship is that the church's name gives credibility and a discussion-starter for the team at festivals, while the Biznistry is free to make its own decisions on how to disburse profits.

Now that the sparks have settled into a cozy fireplace, the church and its Biznistry have a good relationship. As the congregation sees the outreach opportunities the profits have made possible, more members are getting involved, volunteering to serve at the busy kettle corn booth at weekend festivals. But some church members still aren't behind the Biznistry idea. When Jim invited one of the invitees of the initial breakfasts to share his talents by joining their leadership team, the answer was, "Absolutely not." This member was just as passionate as Jim that the church should be pleasing to God; his understanding was just different. Pastor Val believes some members are uncomfortable with the enterprise because it represents pretty radical, out-of-the-box thinking. Other people don't like taking risks and find change difficult. "They either didn't understand the vision, or didn't catch the vision," says Pastor Val. "But they do buy Kettle Corn."

Go and Be

It's not easy to put Biznistry into the four walls of the church, as the Lindenwald Church's experience demonstrates. Recently a member of At Work On Purpose asked Chuck Proudfit at a roundtable discussion what would be the easiest way to reach more believers to grow the organization. "Theoretically, we should go to where they gather—the local church," Chuck responded. "It all makes sense; it's like a watering hole. But when you get close, you discover it's surrounded by barbed wire, and it's electric. So you get pricked, and you get electrocuted."

An electric fence around the church? Certainly no pastor or congregation would allow this. Yet Christians and others who approach the local church with new ideas often find invisible barbed wire. As we have seen, even the church has often bought into the Greek notion of a sacred/secular separation, which may cause an otherwise open-minded congregation to question the wisdom of Biznistry. Whether a church's reluctance to embrace an idea takes the form of ecclesiastical red tape, suspicion, hostility, or apathy, the result may be that a church can unknowingly drive away the very ones God is using to advance his Kingdom.

Innovation often grates against tradition, and Biznistry challenges the tradition of how local churches have typically conducted ministry. When a congregation in our area outgrew its old building, they built a beautiful new one with a round sanctuary and bright, contemporary furnishings. The church was understandably proud of its new building, so they installed a message on the wall facing the street: "Come and see." Their heart was in the right place: they wanted to reach out to their community and invite others to experience God's love in their new home. The inscription, however, expresses in a few words a traditional approach to ministry that not only is becoming less relevant in today's world but also falls short of what Jesus taught by word and example.

In the short three years of Jesus' earthly ministry, we have no record of him ever inviting people to come to where he was staying for Bible study or healing; we do have many examples of him going to others' homes. He taught in the temple, but he also taught outside the temple. He traveled to where the people were—even if it meant going places where traditional religious people didn't go. Consider again the Great Commission: "Go and make disciples, teaching them . . ."[17] Jesus spoke not to nonbelievers, saying "Come and See," but to believers, instructing them to "Go"—and Be. For how does a believer "make disciples"? By being a Christ-like example. The apostle Paul told the Corinthian church, "I am not seeking my own good but the good of many, so that they may be saved. Follow my example, as I follow the example of Christ."[18]

If the church is to embrace the Faith at Work movement, including Biznistry, it must exchange the traditional "Come and See" approach to ministry for the more biblical strategy of "Go and Be." The church now stands at a critical crossroads. It can seize this opportunity to claim the marketplace for Christ, or it can do nothing and allow the devil to control this huge area of what should be God's Kingdom. More than changing music or worship style, adding Bible classes or updating church programs, a revival in marketplace ministry would have a greater lasting Kingdom impact than in any other area of the church, largely because of the vast amount of marketplace resources and the large amount of time we spend there.

Perhaps the church's reluctance to change is one reason for the recent explosion of parachurch organizations focusing on marketplace ministry. Another reason may be that Christians who want to live for God in the marketplace don't get wrapped up in the denominationalism that characterizes the church today. They're interested in supporting each other or getting a prayer group started in the work environment, not in convincing others to share their view on predestination or eschatology. Whatever the reason for the primary growth being outside the organized church, the reality is that the Spirit is moving, lives are being transformed in the marketplace, and the church risks becoming a dinosaur that doesn't understand until it starts to lose people and money to parachurch organizations.

For example, Bob Buford and his Halftime organization have focused on a relatively new resource: those over age 50 who have become financially independent and want to use their gifts and acquired skills to advance God's Kingdom. We've seen how Pete West is living this out in his work with Self Sustaining Enterprises. Imagine how other men and women could "change careers" and be used in the local church to serve Christ!

Biznistry can release institutional churches from the confines of their worship centers, and make them more relevant and vital to their communities. Biznistry professionals serve as missionaries to the marketplace, reaching people for Christ who would never enter the four walls of a local church, but can be reached for eternity through the marketplace. We believe that marketplace ministry, in its many forms including Biznistry, is one of the most significant ministry frontiers of the 21st century. But at the same time, the Biznistry journey is one of restoration. It helps us recreate the exciting conditions of the early church, where marketplace and ministry were inseparably intertwined, and ministry had expression 24/7.

Is God moving you and your church to consider Biznistry? You will surely ask if it is God's will for your congregation. The best way to know God's will is to study his heart. We see his heart in the Sheep and Goats metaphor, where he shows that his love for "the least of these" is so great he considers our service to the needy as service to Christ himself. Put this together with the Parable of the Talents, also recorded in Matthew 25, and we see that God expects us to put all our talents, abilities, and gifts to work in serving the truly needy, thereby serving God.

We know that the vast majority of the world's material resources—money, talent, equipment, and facilities—are locked up in the marketplace, and that these resources can transform the world when they are better stewarded for Kingdom work. A church that embraces Biznistry opens its hands to accept all the resources God has provided to serve the "least of these," and ultimately serve Christ himself.

The physical and spiritual need in the world today may seem overwhelming, but God has equipped us with all we need for battle. Isn't all this an opportunity, as it once was for David,[19] to serve God's purposes in our generation? God's people, the church, can continue with the status quo, reaching some for Christ and shaking their heads in defeat for the multitudes who fall into disease, despair and death, casualties of the battle against apathy and evil. Or the church can follow Joshua's example, embracing unorthodox plans for battle, expecting God to follow through where he leads to accomplish great things for him.

Notes

[1] Matthew 25:14-30

[2] Matthew 22:37-39

[3] Matthew 28:18-20

[4] Ephesians 1:22-23

[5] Acts 16:14

[6] Acts 18:2-3; Romans 16:3

[7] I Corinthians 14:26

[8] Ephesians 4:11

[9] Ephesians 4:16

[10] Romans 14:8

[11] I Thessalonians 4:11

[12] Acts 2:47

[13]I Peter 3:15

[14]Matthew 28:19

[15]Colossians 3:23

[16]I Peter 4:10

[17]Matthew 28:19

[18]I Corinthians 10:33 – 11:1

[19]Acts 13:36

6

Peril . . . and Promise

Where the battle rages, there the loyalty of the soldier is proved.
–Martin Luther

Are you ready to dive into Biznistry? Not so fast. Biznistry is difficult, and can even be treacherous. It's part of this vast movement of God we call marketplace ministry, and every campaign of God requires warriors fully committed to the cause, dressed in full armor and wielding a sword. Biznistry holds all the promise we've discussed in the preceding chapters, and certainly much more. But it also holds peril for those who enter the battle unprepared or not fully committed.

So if you're serious about this, and we hope you are, let's talk about the hard stuff.

Are You Ready for Battle?

First, look in the mirror, and ask yourself: Do I consistently strive to live out my Christian faith even when I'm at work?

We have seen that Biznistry knocks down the wall between sacred and secular and puts our faith at the center of all we do. For some Christians, that sacred/secular divide may serve as a convenient excuse for not being fully dedicated to Christ when they are in the work world. Am I committed to serving Christ in all I do, working for him rather than for personal gain or approval of others?

Foundational to Biznistry is the concept that we are not owners of our resources, but stewards. God has equipped us with all the gifts, talents, and resources we need to be successful in the marketplace, but only if we recognize they all are his, not ours. Biznistry requires taking a chance with our resources not to make ourselves rich, but to advance the Kingdom. This is sacrificial, and directly contrary to the methods of traditional business.

In Biznistry we are working not for transitory treasures on earth, but for eternal treasure in heaven. We cannot have a divided purpose; "no one can serve two masters." The reason God gives for this is simple: "Where your treasure is, there your heart will be also."[1] Matching our heart with God's goes hand-in-hand with working for his Kingdom rather than our own.

Practically speaking, this can be scary. God's vision for an enterprise is often infinitely greater than our own, because he is "able to do immeasurably more than all we ask or imagine."[2] If God reveals his full vision to us, we may feel overwhelmed; we doubtless will have no idea how to accomplish it on our own. If he doesn't reveal it to us all at once (and this is more common) we may be unsure of our ultimate goal, having to take only one step at a time as God directs. In either case, our faith in God must be unwavering so we are led by him rather than by our own understanding.

God is our commander-in-chief and we are soldiers on a battlefield when we're claiming the marketplace for God. Most people still hold the Greek philosophy of separating work and faith, including many well-meaning Christians. There will be resistance and even counterattack when you carry Christ into the marketplace, and not only from people. Satan, too, will do all he can to stop the advance of God's Kingdom. Just look at the present spiritual deadness in the marketplace, and you'll realize how important it was for him to take control of this area in the first place. The marketplace, however, is not by rights his; it is territory we as Christians should be liberating and claiming, because it belongs to God.

This is not safe territory. Persecution is entirely possible, just as it was for the early church. We are fast becoming a post-Christian society, and all of us have seen unbelievers launch attacks on the Christian faith. We shouldn't be surprised if these attacks increase, especially as Christians move to reclaim territory that has fallen to Satan.

There are potential perils of the more mundane variety as well. We know, because we fell into some of them early in our development of Biznistry. One of these was diversifying before we were ready, starting too many enterprises too soon. We also made some costly legal and financial mistakes. We're very thankful that God was in control, and the enterprises that turned out to be poor choices for us were spun off to other Christian entrepreneurs who could invest the time and skill necessary for success. One of our reasons for writing this book and developing the in-depth workshops and training that follow is to help others learn from our experience and avoid our early mistakes.

The Heart of the King

If serving in Biznistry can be so perilous, why in the world would anyone decide to leave the relatively safe and comfortable world of traditional business and knowingly take on such a challenge? And when struggles come, and they will, or failure knocks us to the ground, what makes Biznistry workers keep getting up and facing more of the same?

The answer is passion—passion for the heart of God. In the previous chapter we looked at God's heart in Matthew 25, and saw that it is firmly centered on the "least of these"—those who suffer from poverty and disease and injustice, those who cannot fight for themselves. They're the 2.5 billion people in the world who live on less than U.S. $2 a day. They're the 8 million children under age 5 who die each year from preventable causes. They're the millions of people who have stopped dreaming of a better future because of war, famine, and catastrophe.[3]

Overwhelming? Maybe. But also consider this: we are making progress. Child deaths have been halved over the last few decades thanks to better nutrition, health care, and standards of living, according to the World Bank. The proportion of the world's population with access to clean drinking water increased from 76% to 86% from 1990 to 2006. In 1990, 13 million children in developing countries died before the age of 5 from diseases such as diarrhea, malnutrition, pneumonia, AIDS, malaria, and tuberculosis. By 2006 that number had dropped to 10 million. And more children are going to school than ever before.[4] Persistence and passion are paying off in saved lives—but there is a long way to go. We continue to fight for the "least of these" because they are so near to God's heart that God views our service to them as service to himself.

The "least of these" are individuals, each created in the image of God for a purpose. One of them is the 12-year-old girl in Nigeria who can't go to school because she must walk for hours each day to fetch water for her family. During those long walks, she carries not only the weight of several full containers, but also the fear of rape or abduction by men who prey on the women and girls who are most often the water-carriers of the villages. There's also the Sub-Saharan woman whose husband has died of AIDS, searching for some way to provide for her four young children. But the least of these are closer to home, too. A former drug addict in your community wants a second chance to lead a productive life. An abused child on your street wonders if she has any worth, and where she can look for hope. The least of these are around the world and in your own city, and each of them is dear to the heart of God. He is our Master, our General; and he is the one who calls us into battle.

If God is our only Master, then our loyalty belongs only to him—and it's this fierce loyalty that fuels our passion. Robert the Bruce was a king who inspired such loyalty in his people, even after his death. Erwin McManus, in his book *The Barbarian Way*, shows how this loyalty drove an outmanned army into fierce battle:

Robert the Bruce was the Scottish noble whose character is most remembered for betraying William Wallace, but he later rose up to lead Scotland to freedom after Wallace's execution. He died in 1329 at the age of 54. Shortly before his death, Robert the Bruce requested that his heart be removed from his body and taken on crusade by a worthy knight. James Douglas, one of his closest friends, was at his bedside and took on the responsibility. The heart of Robert the Bruce was embalmed and placed in a small container that Douglas carried around his neck. In every battle that Douglas fought, he literally carried the heart of his king pressed against his chest.

In the early spring of 1330, Douglas sailed from Scotland to Granada, Spain, and engaged in a campaign against the Moors. In an ill-fated battle, Douglas found himself surrounded, and in this situation death was both certain and imminent. In that moment Douglas reached for the heart strapped around his neck, flung the heart into the enemy's midst, and cried out, "Fight for the heart of your king!" One historian quoted Douglas as shouting, "Forward, brave heart, as ever thou were wont to do, and Douglas will follow his king's heart or die!" The motto of the Douglas clan to which the present duke belongs is even to this day simply, "Forward."

Although anyone who understands the heart of God knows that the Crusades were a tragic lesson in missing the point, the power of this story awakens within me a primal longing that I am convinced waits to be unleashed within everyone who is a follower of Jesus Christ. To belong to God is to belong to his heart. If we have responded to the call of Jesus to leave everything and follow him, then there is a voice within us crying out, "Fight for the heart of your King!"[5]

That's what we need to do—fight for the heart of our King. This is what drives us, what gets us back on our feet when we fall. We may be bludgeoned and bloody, but we get up and go on because we're fighting for the heart of our King. Unless we understand God's heart for the poor and oppressed, unless we allow ourselves to enter into the suffering of others—unless we follow God's heart—we will not have the drive necessary to fight this battle.

The need is so great we're not sure where to start. We feel like wimpy warriors with the odds firmly against us—Joshua at the battle of Jericho, David facing Goliath, or Gideon and his band of 300 facing the powerful army of Midian. To attack this immense problem will take out-of-the-box solutions, but that's nothing new for God's people. Our strategy, like theirs, may be unorthodox, but that's our heritage. Like David, Joshua, and Gideon, we don't need to be strong in ourselves to win battles; we *do* need to be strong in our faith. God told Gideon, who protested that he was the least in his family within the weakest clan of Manasseh, "Go in the strength you have," and promised "I will be with you."[6] God then culled Gideon's forces, permitting those who "tremble with fear" to turn back.[7] He wanted to ensure that victory would be seen as his rather than by human strength. Gideon and his small band then moved forward to victory, relying not on their physical strength, but on God's faithfulness and power.

To impact the immense suffering we see in our world will take that kind of faith, a faith that not only believes in God but trusts in him. It will take a faith that leads us out of our comfortable Christian existence. It will take an innovative movement of people with relentless passion, a global community of Christ followers awakening imagination, igniting passion and unleashing purpose. Our outrage needs to stretch beyond emotion.

Clearly, we are following God's heart into a spiritual battle; but we are also in an economic battle. How do we attack the problems of education, healthcare and nutrition on an economic level? How do we attack pockets of poverty around the world? How do we give those in need a hand up not just a handout? How do we help them build a sustainable future?

This is an area where Biznistry can serve as a military specialist. If we're battling for nothing less than the lives of people and the heart of God, we need to enlist every believer to serve. As we have seen, Biznistry uses resources the traditional church often cannot, or does not, tap; its recognition that every talent and treasure comes from God and is meant to be used in his service provides a wealth of tools and weapons in the economic armory.

Biznistry measures its success in profits made available for ministry; it also measures its success in changed lives. Every day Biznistries see evidence of victory when they use innovation to launch transformation. At Green Recycling Works, former addicts are now living for Christ and gaining the training and experience to become productive in the marketplace. In Nigeria, children are healthy and attending school because their village now has its own deep-water well.

And in Biznistries everywhere, men and women are learning each day how to minister to those around them as they work.

Imagine a marketplace where Christians operate with a biblical worldview, where they take to heart the concept that there is no sacred/secular divide, only the sacred and sinful. Imagine all the variety of resources in the marketplace harnessed to serve God's Kingdom. We could tear down strongholds that wall out Christ, and liberate the marketplace and its resources for God's work. The peril is real, but the promise is immeasurably greater.

Transforming the Next Generation

Transforming the marketplace begins by transforming people. And it takes every one of us—people of all backgrounds, ages and abilities; people with God's heart, committed to serving him in all we do. Transformation is lasting when it becomes part of a community's culture, modeled and passed on from one generation to the next.

When we talk about transforming the next generation, we're talking about discipleship. Churches and parachurch ministries understand the importance of reaching out to nonbelievers and encouraging Christians on high school and college campuses, but as students graduate they are left to find their own way in a marketplace largely devoid of godly example. Biznistry provides role models and daily discipleship for young Christians, teaching them *by example* how to worship and serve God while at work. But first we need to reach out and bring them in.

Generation Y has flung open the doors of the marketplace and marched in with habits, attitudes, and expectations very different from those of their older counterparts. They're looking for opportunities to develop personally and in their careers; they crave flexibility and innovation; and they want their work to do more than provide for themselves and their families—they also want it to make a difference in the wider world.

At the recent annual Kairos summit, where 350 young entrepreneurs pitched their ideas to business executives and political leaders, a social mission was central to almost every idea. Ankur Jain, the 22-year-old founder of the Kairos Society, explained that the youngest members of the workforce are often more motivated by social good than wealth. "They see success as changing lives," he said.[8]

Social enterprise is a hot trend, and many Gen Yers will be attracted to the sense of purpose it provides, allowing them to "do well by doing good." As we have seen, Biznistry offers a Christ-focused alternative that reaches beyond the good to the Great (Commandment and Commission). But like any business, Biznistry must adapt to the needs of the next generation of workers, providing both fuel and focus for their passion.

For the first time in history, the marketplace comprises four generations of workers, bringing with them a vast array of experience, skills, and ideas. Biznistry has special appeal to entrepreneurs of all ages, and holds power to transform our youngest workers into an army of Christ-followers changing the world. Most Biznistries are small enterprises, and they thrive on innovation. We've seen how half-timers, those around mid-life who want to move beyond success to significance in their work lives, often fit well in a Biznistry model. Older workers, too, retired from a previous career with much more to contribute, may be called to Biznistry. Men and women spanning the age spectrum working side by side, along with Biznistry's emphasis on growing people, creates fertile ground for the kind of personal and career development that Gen Yers want and need.

Young Christians entering the marketplace have desires similar to other Gen Yers, but those truly in love with the Lord understand they are stewards of their resources, and want to use their work to glorify God. The best way for them to learn to do this is from Christians already in the marketplace who consistently live for Christ in all they do. "Adults should model a life devoted to God," says Grant Rolfer, a twenty-something minister to college students. "Christ should pour from them. The logistics of the workplace model will naturally follow."

Here at Grace Chapel, we've invested more than a decade in developing a *culture* of Biznistry—an environment where entrepreneurs thrive, and where young people see and experience the integration of faith and work. One way we do this is by pastors and staff focusing not only on the spiritual and emotional pulse of the church, but on its talents and skills as well. We can direct new people toward business contacts in the body of Christ, and steer them toward opportunities for using their gifts and skills in the church. We talk about all of us being ministers, serving the Lord at home, in the community, and in the marketplace, as well as "at church."

Another way we develop this culture of Biznistry is through our Innovate group, a regular gathering where young entrepreneurs can develop their ideas and skills. One talented young musician wanted to give guitar lessons and send his profits to our well-digging Biznistry in Nigeria, using a Web site to advertise. He had no expertise or passion for marketing, but needed traffic on his site to launch his Biznistry. Through Innovate he has connected with others who are helping him with the administrative and marketing aspects of his business, so he can thrive as an entrepreneurial musician.

Will Housh, founder of the Housh, Inc. group of e-commerce enterprises, strives to create a culture of giving while merging faith and work within his business. One way he does this is by offering his employees an annual all-expenses paid company trip to a Back2Back Ministry international site Will's Biznistry supports. As his team members work at children's homes and interact with the kids, they not only realize how their work at Housh, Inc.

impacts the needy, but also develop a passion to give and serve.

Our goal should be to create a culture where merging work and faith is the norm rather than the exception. We will know we've done our part in transforming the next generation of Christians in the marketplace when we can say with Paul: "We continually remember before our God and Father your work produced by faith, your labor prompted by love, and your endurance inspired by hope in our Lord Jesus Christ. . . . You know how we lived among you for your sake. You became imitators of us and of the Lord."[9]

Continuing Construction

We've been creating a culture of Biznistry for more than a decade, but we're still pioneers. As a vibrant, emerging frontier with its roots in apostolic times, marketplace ministry has become the arena for one of the most significant spiritual battles of our generation. Isn't this a battle worth waging? Blowing trumpets while walking in circles is an unorthodox way to topple a city wall. Integrating faith and work is not the norm, either, in today's world. But throughout history, God has challenged his people to listen, to obey, and to walk in faith where he leads, using whatever resources he has put in our hands. We hope you will join us in the battle against the ungodly separation of work and faith, and fight to claim the vast resources of the marketplace for the Kingdom of God.

To get involved and learn more, you will find a list of resources at the end of this chapter. At Work On Purpose, the vibrant faith-at-work ministry founded by Chuck Proudfit, spans the marketplace, offering support to workers in the traditional marketplace and to those involved in Biznistry. This organization is a good first contact.

Above all, don't go it alone. Ask anyone in Biznistry, and they will tell you a major key to success is surrounding yourself with other Christians who share a passion for your Biznistry's purpose, but bring a wide variety of skills, especially in areas where you are not strong. Remember, a Biznistry functions as the body of Christ, and each part serves a needed function. So please contact us.

This book was designed to introduce you to the "what" and "why" of Biznistry. Your next step may be the new video series focusing on the "how" of Biznistry, helping you make specific plans for your enterprise. Please contact At Work On Purpose for information about this series. We invite pastors with questions about Biznistry and the church to contact Jeff Greer.

Notes

[1]Matthew 6: 19-24

[2]Ephesians 3:20

[3]"Poverty Overview," The World Bank, accessed 10/20/12.
    <http://www.worldbank.org/en/topic/poverty/overview>

[4]*Ibid.*

[5]Erwin McManus, *The Barbarian Way.* Thomas Nelson, 2005.

[6]Judges 6:14-16

[7]Judges 7:1-3

[8]Nate C. Hindman, "For Young Entrepreneurs, Social Mission
    Trumps Money," *Huffington Post,* Feb. 13, 2012.
    <http://www.huffingtonpost.com/2012/02/13/young-
    entrepreneurs_n_1272488.html?ref=small-business-news-and-
    trends>

[9]I Thessalonians 1:3, 5-6

Contact Information

At Work On Purpose and Chuck Proudfit

9891 Montgomery Road #202

Cincinnati, OH 45242

www.atworkonpurpose.org

(800) 513-9580

Grace Chapel and Pastor Jeff Greer

406 Fourth Avenue

Mason, OH 45040

Phone: (513) 754-0333

www.grace-chapel.com

Self Sustaining Enterprises

404 Fourth Avenue

Mason, OH 45044

Phone: (513) 234-7898

www.sseinc.org

Made in the USA
San Bernardino, CA
01 September 2018